The Fiction of

J.D.SALINGER

A Study in the Concept of Man

The Fiction of
J.D. SALINGER
A Study in the Concept of Man

Subhash Chandra

Sangam Books

SANGAM BOOKS LIMITED
57 London Fruit Exchange
Brushfield Street
London E1 6EP, U.K.

By arrangement with
PRESTIGE BOOKS
3/28, East Patel Nagar
New Delhi 110 008

Published by Sangam Books Limited, 2000

ISBN 0 86132 424 2

Composed by Vivek Mathur, Delhi 110 006 Ph. 3981867
Printed by Dhawan Industries Offset, New Delhi 110 028

Contents

Foreword

J.D. Salinger was one of the most popular novelists of the fifties and the sixties in America. Students on the campuses in America went around with a copy of *The Catcher in the Rye* and/or Rilke's *Duino Elegies*. The campus dialect was generously sprinkled with Holdenisms. Critics of the American Novel called the period, the age of Holden. Instead of capitalizing on this boom, however, Salinger became a recluse and withdrew from society as if the "phoniness" of the world had finally got to him. He was one of the novelists I was working on in the early sixties in the United States, and I tried several times to get in touch with him. But all I got by way of a response was sepulchral silence.

Dr. Subhash Chandra's study is an admirable attempt at understanding the complexity and depth of the concept of man in Salinger's fiction. Salinger's best known character, Holden Caulfield, represents what he thinks of man in the modern world. He functions in a dystopian world of hypocrisy, philistinism, acquisitiveness, promiscuity and moral degradation. What saves him from mental destruction is his capacity for love and compassion expressed in his desire to be a catcher in the rye saving children from falling over "the edge of some crazy cliff." His compassion, however, doesn't interfere with his critical faculty and sense of discrimination. He is probably the greatest detector of phoniness in all modern fiction. He is completely turned off by the phoney "adultism" around him even to the point of a nervous breakdown. One of his tutors passes on to him a significant insight *a la* Wilhelm Stekel, "The mark of the immature man is that he wants to die nobly for a cause while the mark of the mature man is that he wants to live humbly for one."

Readers of American fiction of the mid-twentieth century will find this book enjoyable and useful. It is well written, insightful and convincingly argued.

ISAAC SEQUEIRA
Former Professor of English
Osmania University
Hyderabad

For

my mother

Preface

With the publication of *The Catcher in the Rye*, J.D. Salinger evoked extensive critical response which continued when his later fiction appeared. The Salinger criticism largely concerns itself with themes of initiation, alienation and whether the protagonists in Salinger's fiction are saints and pilgrims or freaks, fakes and phonies, like the people they condemn. In other words, the critical opinion mainly deals with individual aspects of the concept of man by analyzing the mental make-up of the major Salinger protagonists. A comprehensive work, focussing on Salinger's concept of man as it is revealed in the corpus of his writings, does not exist. The present book seeks to examine Salinger's fiction with a view to ascertaining the concept of man in its totality, as it emerges from the body of his writings.

The book traces the novelists's concept of man through the following works: *The Early Stories* (1940-48), *The Catcher in the Rye* (1951), *Nine Stories* (1953), *Franny and Zooey* (1961), *Raise High the Roof Beam, Carpenters; and Seymour: An Introduction* (1963) and long story, "Hapworth 16, 1924," which appeared in *The New Yorker* (1965). Besides analyzing the textual narratives to find out the nature of predicaments Salinger's major protagonists are faced with, the study also considers the values which help them not only to confront the dystopian reality, but also to lead a conscious and meaningful life in the midst of such a reality. Salinger's efforts to invest his protagonists with a set of values and make them cherish certain ideals amidst prevailing corruption and moral squalor in society, constitute his concept of man. It is through these values that the major protagonists perform a journey from melancholia and despair to joy and hope; from innocence and insouciance to maturity and acceptance of reality, and assumption of social responsibility, and succeed in discerning a great contrast between beauty, dream, love and spiritual maximalism on the one hand and what Holden calls "phoney" on the other. Preserving the integrity and dignity of the self, while remaining an integral part of society and assuming social responsibility become the credo of the Salinger heroes.

I express my gratitude to Dr. V.K. Roy, for examining the manuscript with critical attention. His unstinted moral support and guidance took me out of many academic cul-de-sacs, I inevitably ran into, during the course of writing this book. I am grateful to Dr. B.S. Goyal for some fresh insights into Salinger's fiction. I am also grateful to Professor Marshall W. Fishwick and Dr. Unmeel B. Mehta for sending me from the United States some Salinger criticism and some of the early stories of Salinger, not available in India. I shall remain obliged to my friend and colleague, Mr. C. Chintamani, a voracious reader, who introduced me to Salinger, and who allowed me to use the vast resources of his personal library. I need to thank my wife, Nilima Chandra, not only for cheerfully reading the proofs, but also making some insightful suggestions and my son Apoorva Chandra, for sportingly bearing the neglect during the period of my preoccupation with the project. Thanks are due to Dr. K.B. Razdan and Dr. Manorama Trikha for their valuable guidance, and to Dr. R.S. Avana for his help. And not the least my mother, in her silent way, acted as a catalyst in my taking up and completing the project.

I am indebted to the American Studies Research Centre, Hyderabad, for helping me in collecting research materials for this project from their vast library resources and enabling me to visit the Centre several times at their expense. I also thank the American Centre Library, Delhi, for their help.

SUBHASH CHANDRA

Introduction

The presence and operation of certain forces in society inevitably lead to continuing tension between man and his ambience. Man vis-a-vis society became a recurrent theme, dominating American imagination with its transition from the imitative to the optative phase. Among the early men of letters, it was James Fenimore Cooper who, with the creation of Natty Bumppo in his 'Leather-Stocking Tales,' gave the figure of an American protagonist as an individual catering to purely native needs and situations. The response of Cooper's hero to the corruption of civilization was rejection of society. By the mid-nineteenth century, industrial and technological advancement gave rise to the creed of material acquisitiveness and hedonism. This resulted in the erosion of moral and spiritual values, making the corruption and dehumanization more intense and widespread.

Feeling threatened in this stifling and circumscribing social milieu, the nineteenth century American self became obsessed with safeguarding its freedom and integrity. The Americanness of the American protagonist made him a man on the run, asserting his non-conformity to the value-orientation and institutionalized conventions of the civilized society. Writers like Herman Melville and Mark Twain, in particular, conceived of self in flight from society, and their works came to dramatize the revulsion of the protagonists against a corrupt and degenerate society. Ishmael's flight to the sea whenever he finds himself "growing grim about the mouth," and whenever "it is damp, drizzly November" (Melville 1962:1) in his soul, and Huck's lighting out for the "Territory ahead" symbolize the protagonist's revulsion against a morally corrupt and degenerate society.

The violence, cruelty and madness of military bureaucracy let loose by the two World Wars in the present century turned the contemporary American society into a dystopian hell. Feelings of shock, guilt and despair lacerated man's psyche, making him neurotically apprehensive about the freedom and authenticity of his self. Besides this, power of the state, symbolized by the two wars, the constricting social institutions in the form of the corporation, army and university, and rapid decline in the moral values as a result of increasing commercialism and mercenariness made man's predicament vis-a-vis society still more intractable. The post-Second World War novelists posited protagonists against society in a bid to find a solution to the problem of selves. These protagonists were not always successful; often they got bruised, browbeaten and battered. Many times they took refuge in flight, sex, violence (sadomasochism), drugs or being constantly on the run.

The heroes of the post-Second World War novels such as those of Saul Bellow, William Styron, John Updike and Bernard Malamud display affirmation—howsoever tentative or ambiguous—in spite of moral degeneration and ennui everywhere. J.D. Salinger also belongs to this humanistic tradition: his works show a prominent concern with the concept of man with a view to finding a solution to man's predicament in the contemporary American dystopia.

II

With the publication of his early stories from 1940 onwards, Salinger evoked a lively critical debate. However, *The Catcher in the Rye* (1951) resulted in such an extensive critical response that George Steiner summed it up, though pejoratively, as "The Salinger Industry" (1959:360-68), and the decade came to be called "'the age of Holden'" (French 1963:36)—the hero of the novel. The critical attention paid to Salinger continued to be extensive in the later years when he got published his works like *Nine Stories* (1953), *Franny and Zooey* (1961), *Raise High the Roof Beam, Carpenters; and Seymour: An Introduction* (1963), and the long story "Hapworth 16, 1924" (1965).

The critical response to Salinger's works has been variegated. Critics have interpreted his fictional works from diverse points of view. Frederick Gwynn and Joseph Blotner in their monograph consider "For Esme—with Love and Squalor" as the high point of his art and interpret Salinger's fiction as delineating the "basic human conflict between love and what Salinger's Esme calls Squalor" (1958:3). James E. Miller, Jr., who puts Salinger in "the pre-eminent position" among the post-Second World War novelists, views Salinger's fiction as works of affirmation in which the characters transcend "the modern wasteland and its agony" (1965:45). The opinion held by Warren French is diametrically opposite to that of Miller. Placing "Uncle Wiggily in Connecticut" at the centre of Salinger's fiction, he asserts that it is a "phoney" world which triumphs over the "nice" world, as the "basic concepts of perishability of the 'nice' world and the 'phoniness' of the persisting world provide the warp and woof on which Salinger weaves." (French 1963:46) his fiction. The strangeness of gestures made by Salinger's protagonists is taken note of by Ihab Hassan, who interprets Salinger's fiction as a conflict between "the Assertive Vulgarian" and "the Responsive Outsider" (1961:261). According to him Salinger, through the corpus of his fiction, "has kept faith with the redeeming powers of outrage and compassion." (289) Also talking about the "strange, quixotic gesture," (262) Hassan says that it becomes an act of affirmation of the fictional hero when pitted against a dull and angry world. Bracketting Salinger with Updike, Styron, and Bellow, David D. Galloway (1981:209) regards Salinger as an absurdist writer whose characters re-enter the world. Ostensibly, Galloway identifies love as the main instrument of re-entry into society. Richard Boyd Hauck also, like Galloway, views Salinger in the tradition of the absurd. He, too, believes that Salinger's protagonists succeed in finding a solution to their predicaments, arising out of the absurdity of the world (1971:241). For James Lundquist, Salinger's writings represent "pilgrim's progress" culminating into moments of revelation for the characters in the later works. Lundquist believes that Salinger highlights the state of emptiness resulting from lack of belief in God and tells man how this state can be "treated and alleviated" (1979:4-5).

Eberhard Alsen, (1983:xi-xii) however, concerns himself with the Glass stories. Treating the Glass stories as a composite novel, he pinpoints two themes: Buddy's struggle to understand Seymour by writing about him or in other words, artist's quest to understand his mission and to find the right form for his work and Seymour's quest for God. Alsen opines that Salinger being a Neo-Romantic writer, his fiction reflects the "hopes and aspirations" of the age rather than "its fears and doubts" and reveals "a transcendent meaning behind the appearances of everyday life." (251-53) As against this, Howard M. Harper Jr., (1967:195) sees characters in the novelist's fiction being in the process of learning that in trying to become more than human by withdrawing into spirituality, they inevitably become less than human. While Harper sees some hope for the heroes, Philip Roth finds them spurning the life "as it is lived in this world, in this reality" (1969:3-5) and remarks that Salinger does not provide an answer to the problem of living in this world.

Benjamin De Mott gives a different colour to the "Silence" Salinger's protagonists observe against the word-mongers by terming it as "a strategy and sacrament." It becomes a strategy by devaluing "the chatter of Lane Coutells" (1969:220) who are figures of phony authority and competence and sacrament inasmuch as it is a "protest against selfishness and for organic existence." (219)

Alfred Kazin (1969:121) considers Salinger as an American writer with lean resources for his writing material, having to explore, "personality" or the "'mystery of personality" instead of the drama of social existence. Neither is Kazin (1962:50) impressed by the Glasses who are lost in "self love." Helen Weinberg, on the contrary, affirms that Salinger's fiction represents "a vision of hope and carries with it a celebration of life," (1970:143) because the novelist regards the self as being full of potential for love, compassion and goodness. Donald Barr goes a step further in calling Salinger's protagonists "Saints, pilgrims and artists," who find themselves in hell, suffering and without escape (1964:538-41).

Talking about Holden Caulfield, Jerry H. Bryant brings out the romantic stance of the boy-hero who associates "adulthood with phoniness, phoniness with change and change with death" and never comes to the stage of mature affirmation (1970:239). Carl F. Strauch also compares Salinger's characters to Romantics. He finds them sharing the "capacity to feel and suffer" with the Romantics and considers this as "representative of the human condition." (1963:40) John Russell (1966:299-306) provides an interesting insight into Salinger's heroes by noticing recurrent references to the "feet" of the main personages. His contention is that Salinger's mature fiction yields meaning in terms of "human feet": crossed legs with drawn-in feet connoting self-enclosed, selfish individuals and dangling legs with exposed feet symbolizing generosity and altruism. Constant references to feet bring out the novelist's faith in the "non-cerebral"—feet being the farthest from the ratiocinative faculty.

Jack Ludwig criticizes the protagonists for their feeling of isolation resulting from their peculiar attitudes towards reality and goes on to accuse Salinger of creating "artistic dirty pool" by peopling the world with shams and then concluding that "it is full of shams" (1962:30-31). Analyzing the predicaments faced by the novelist's heroes, Sisir Kumar Ghose (1965:49) regards them as "maladjusted." Almost everyone of them carries a "private vision." Each one, according to Ghose, fails to realize the dream, though the dreamer survives in most cases. Sidney Finkelstein (1968:219-25) follows Ghose, but with a little difference. He also points out the "psychological estrangement" of Holden Caulfield and the Glass heroes. However, according to him, the cause of the alienation is not a "private vision" but disgust for a "phoney" and "freakish" society. Warren French (1970:25-28), labelling the 1950s as the "Age of Salinger" also observes that "defeat or death" are the only alternatives that constitute Salinger's vision. K. McSweeny also points out that there is "much excellent social observation" in Salinger, and there is very "little social vision" in his works. The novelist has no "positive, post-puberty alternative" (1978:62) to the world. Alfred Chester's contention is similar to that of McSweeny. He considers the concept of Christian love offered as a mode of survival in an ugly world as wishy-washy. "All Zooey [a character in *Franny and Zooey*] is saying is that if you close your eyes and pretend that Blacks are Whites, then you can love them" (1963:472).

Tom Davis (1963:41-46) regards the influence of Zen Buddhism on the novelist as "harmful" because the solution presented by Zooey, one of the protagonists in *Franny and Zooey*, being an uneasy truce with the squalid reality, is hardly effective. Another critic to take note of Zen Buddhist influence on Salinger is Peter Balbert. But unlike Tom Davis, he extols the qualitative improvement Zen makes in Salinger's works, saying that in the religious ethos of Zen, Salinger gets a "framework for the transcendental serenity Roth desperately seeks and Mailer relentlessly avoids" (1980:74).

According to Paul Levine, the Salinger hero compromises the principle of "social responsibility" by choosing the "private world" over the "public world" (society) to which he refuses to adjust (1962:112). A contrary view is provided by David L. Stevenson (1957:216) who assesses Salinger's heroes as being "alienated" from the quiet interflow of "love and affection," thereby representing the state of man in contemporary America.

According to Dennis L. O'Connor, Salinger is a "writer with serious religious concerns" and belongs to "a venerable American tradition dating from the time of Emerson and the Transcendentalists" (1984:316). Ann Marple discerns the theme of quest for purity in *Franny and Zooey* and regards almost the whole of Salinger's work as falling within this "subterranian theme" (1963:243).

Among those who regard Salinger's heroes as not coming to grips with the intractable and ugly features of the world are Michael Walzer who finds the writer suggesting a "kind of reconciliation with the adult world which is at the same time an evasion of worldliness" (1960:156). and Josephine Hendin who thinks that the typical Salinger hero substitutes nostalgia for the family he had as a boy, for the "sense of responsibility" (1978:115). However, as against the opinions expressed by Walzer, David L. Stevenson and Josephine Hendin, Dan Wakefield (1962:177) makes a perceptive interpretation of the novelist's works. He views the protagonists as embarking on a "search for love" and through love eventually overcoming feelings of revulsion and withdrawal, and entering into the "midst of life." David Lodge also believes that both in the early stories and in the later works, depicting the life of Glass family, the central characters wage a "struggle against alienation." (1975:642). Contrary to this, speaking of Holden Caulfield, the boy-hero of *The Catcher in the Rye*, Granville Hicks (1962:191-93) believes the hero's object to be "The Search for Wisdom" as a means of solving the conflict between "integrity and love."

Pointing to the attraction towards the "child" in American culture, Leslie Fiedler regards it as sign of decadence on account of its containing erotic nuances. He interprets this attraction as a "flight from woman, the family, maturity itself" (1962:219-41) and relates it to the hero, Seymour Glass's attraction towards Sybil in "A Perfect Day for Bananafish." To Maxwell Geismer (1958:195), Salinger speaks for non-conformity, represented in the Ivy League Rebellion of the early Fifties, but Geismer does not tell us what it is.

A different strain about the writer's characters is provided by Irving Malin (1962: 26-34), who considers the protagonists as narcissists, for ever lost in themselves and incapable of having meaningful relations. David Leitch (1962:72) endorses this view, saying that the novelist's characters find almost any contact with people "virtually impossible." A contrary view is expressed by James T. Livingston (1968:132) who observes that in Salinger's works religious convictions become part of a secular experience, leading to affirmation. In addition to having been labelled as narcissists, Salinger's heroes are also accused of being a part of the contemporary American social matrix reflecting the malaise afflicting the affluent upper-middle-class whose members have immersed themselves in material pleasures. Consequently, they have lost touch with other human beings and made themselves socially irresponsible. William Wiegand (1958:6-7) terms this malaise as "banana fever," implying that having glutted themselves, like bananafish, on material pleasures, the protagonists render themselves incapable of assimilation with fellow beings. Having first diagonsed "banana fever" in Seymour, William Wiegand sees all "Salinger invalids" including Holden Caulfield, suffering from this disease.

Brian Way (1962:72) exhibits an extremely hostile view about the Glass family fiction ("A Perfect Day for Bananafish," *Franny and Zooey, Raise High the Roof Beam, Carpenters; and Seymour: An Introduction*), He regards the protagonists as monsters in Salinger's "private zoo," the monsters being the neurotics, the precocious children, "chi-chi eccentrics," "quaint intellectuals" and "half-religious maniacs." In sharp contrast to this, Sam S. Baskett's opinion of the Glasses is laudatory. He finds a double significance in them as "individuals" and as "illustrations" showing "what it is good to do under the sun—at least under the American sun of the mid-twentieth century" (1963:50). This line of thinking culminates in Salinger's protagonists being regarded as embodying significance of love in human relationships. Arthur Mizener looks upon the author's characters holding forth that "no man can survive in isolation and that the only community they have to love is the American community to which they have been committed by a lifetime's involvement" (1962:30-31). Continuing in the laudatory strain, Ann L. Hayes regards the "Glass family" as Salinger's major image of the "power to love." (1963:20)

Thus, it becomes clear that critical opinion largely deals with individual aspects of concept of man by analyzing the mental makeup of the major protagonists and their response to the predicaments they find themselves in.

III

The present work will examine Salinger's fiction with a view to ascertaining the concept of man in its totality, as it emerges from the body of his writings. The focus will be on man vis-a-vis society, including man's predicaments resulting from the nature of the contemporary sociological environment. The framework for the purpose of this study will incorporate the enquiry whether man succeeds in transcending his predicaments, leading to his joy and hope or he fails to do so and ends up in depression and despair. Whether man gets alienated and becomes insouciant or accepts society and assumes social responsibility will also form part of the enquiry. Values upheld by the Salinger hero will also be ascertained to assess his capability to differentiate between beauty and goodness on the one hand and what Holden calls "phoney" on the other. And finally, consideration of these values will eventually determine the nature of the novelist's concept of man.

The methodological procedure adopted in the study will be analytical. The textual narratives of Salinger's works will be analyzed in terms of plot, theme, characterization and imagery which cumulatively project the novelist's vision of man. The works chosen for study are the early stories (1940-1948), *The Catcher in the Rye*

(1951), *Nine Stories* (1953), *Franny and Zooey* (1961), *Raise High the Roof Beam, Carpenters; and Seymour: An introduction* (1963) and "Hapworth 16, 1924" (1965). The individual works will be studied in the order of their publication. In case of certain stories (which appeared in magazines earlier) the years of publication in book form will determine the chronological order of the works.

The Introduction defines the methodological procedure adopted in this study. The next chapter surveys the contemporary literary scene and assesses Salinger's novels in the context of the post-Second World War American fiction. The subsequent chapters present author's biographical details and relate, in brief, Salinger's works to his life. The following chapters arrive at Salinger's concept of man through an analysis of the novelistic requirements: plot, characterization, theme and imagery. The conclusion to the study gathers various strands and findings of the individual chapters and binds them into a unity to present the crux of the concept of man contained in Salinger's fiction.

Contemporary American Fiction and J.D. Salinger

Every era has its own climate of ideas. In this climate the artist must live and, through his own unique personal vision, transform his experiences, into works of art. The Second World War, with its heritage of the German death camps, the bombing of Hiroshima and Nagasaki, the fire-bombing of Dresdan and, in fact, the six-year spectacle of human beings transformed into integers of bestiality, was indeed, a nightmare come true. It was a seemingly terminal betrayal of man by man. Consequently, the contemporary American psyche came to be riven by pervasive guilt. The general atmosphere during the post-Second World War period became that of despair, depression and disillusionment with the social institutions and prevailing ideologies.

American civilization seemed to have become the most predatory ever witnessed. In the Far East there was Vietnam and at home there existed civil discord. Economic imperialism was being practised in Central and South America and greedy hands were trying to seize concessions in remote Turkey and South Africa. Martin Luther King, the practitioner of militant non-violence, aroused violence in the frustrated and spiritually impotent men who tried their best to keep him quiet. He exposed their viciousness until they stooped to murder. The Korean War also had a great impact on the American mind. In the course of this war, intense hysteria got whipped up, something not considered necessary even in the Second World War when fascist brutality was not answered with like-brutality and inhumanity. The conviction governing the incidence of the Korean War expressed itself in the form of a struggle against communism, as communism symbolized barbarism and consequently barbaric acts as a reprisal got justified.

A critic, in his review of Burlingame's *The American Conscience* in *The Nation* (27 April 1957) bemoans the blighted American conscience:

> Where is the American conscience today? The witch trials of the late seventeenth century in New England were the last desperate attempt of the Calvinist Clergy to maintain the "covenant." These persecutions were followed by a wave of public remorse and spiritual reform.
>
> We have had our modern parallels. But what covenants are we maintaining? is the question. . . . Our own purges of guilt by association—mainly with the bad, dead past of the New Deal—have been followed not by remorse so much as apathy and inertia. If the nation does indeed face a crisis of survival, if the major areas of the world are in the throes of revolutionary social change, the American conscience today is paralyzed by its semblance of good fortune outwardly, and by a consuming inner anxiety. (Geismar 1958:34)

David Riesman also makes a searching observation on the political climate in America after 1948, in the 1960 preface to the paperback edition of his book, *The Lonely Crowd,* which had first appeared eleven years before:

> The postwar increase in the size and opulence of the middle class pushed the residual poor and unorganized still further away from political influence. . . . In 1948 political imagination and flexibility, even though rare, could still be reasonably hoped for. . . . Before Korea and McCarthy, foreign policy could still be debated, though of course not without pressure from jingoes, and a story in *Time* or the *New York Times* about Morocco or Pakistan was not almost invariably "angled" in terms of the Cold War and the American bases. We had not yet put ourselves by domestic explication of the struggle with world Communism into the bipartisan deep freeze of the last ten years. (1968:213)

The 50s decade in the United States commencing with the Korean War was presided over by an ineffectual person, President Eisenhower. He was one of the least effective Presidents America got since William Henry Harrison. In the aimlessness and confusion of his thinking, 'Ike' came to stand for the spirit of the period. His regime, when the Congress three-fourths of the time was in control of the opposition party, produced nothing of lasting value except for a magnificent Inter-state Highway System. Even that had to be justified on the grounds of military security, rather than as a contribution to the safety and enjoyment of travel.

The intellectual scene did not present an encouraging picture either. In the sphere of science, the electron became the subject of investigation. David Park writes that the indeterminacy of the electron is "the reflection of a universal property of nature." (1964:45) This new view regards a piece of matter as an isolated, transitory event emphasizing its separateness. This separateness came to characterize man's basic relationship with the world. Another discovery of modern physics added to the grimness of the situation. The entropic view of the universe envisaged gradual levelling off of energy, leading to the inevitable universal destruction by "heat-death." Such unnerving concepts unravelled by science further aggravated man's sense of insecurity and also heightened the gloom regarding the overall human condition.

The traditional view of man's cosmic predicament underwent a change. The American individual had at first believed in the existence of order in the universe and in man himself. The semi-utopian concept of organizing society in harmony with the great chain of being and realizing man's real function in the natural order had gained credence. Human problems were thought to be the result of violations by individuals and groups of this natural order. But failure to make this semi-utopian concept a practical reality gave rise to the awareness and recognition of a dystopian reality. The universe came to be regarded as meaningless and even hostile; the hostile adversary refusing to become identifiable. Man now found himself pitted against an absurd and inimical cosmos.

Even the hard-core tenets of orthodox Christianity came to be of little help in enabling man to find meaning in his life. Every type of ethical and scientific explanation failed to remove an ingrained fear of an alien and hostile universe. Nihilism gradually took the place of faith. Purposelessness became the dominant characteristic of man's cosmic situation.

Consequently, the post-Second World War period came to be described variously as an age of anxiety, an age of schism in the soul, a time when man suffers not only from war, persecution, famine and ruin but also from inner problems equally terrible: despair, a conviction of isolation, randomness, meaninglessness in his very existence. Strangely enough, the feeling of despair and the conviction of meaninglessness, appear to trouble man most not under conditions of war, persecution, famine, and ruin but under circumstances of material prosperity.

It came to be argued that Americans were living in a time relatively uncongenial to the making of optative literature. The post-Second World War era seemed to discourage the operative faculties of a creative artist. The world of the young novelists was the same which their predecessors had discovered. The traditional themes that energized the novel in its infancy ceased to be dramatically operative in the post-Second World War novel. Nor were those themes available to the contemporary novel—at least in the same condition that invested them with such great importance in the novel. In this period, so far as the novel dealt with social or political questions, it chose only between a cheery or a sour democratism. In psychology the novel relied either on a mechanical or a clinical use of psychiatry or on the insights established by novelists five decades ago. The young writers of this period came through a war, which was more profoundly disturbing than the first, but the illusions and causes of war, having been once lost, could not be re-lost. The three most memorable novels to emerge from the last war seem to be Norman Mailer's *The Naked and the Dead*, John Horne Burns's *The Gallery* and James Jones's *From Here to Eternity* (its subject matter is military and it closes with the bombing of Pearl Harbor). Speaking of the younger novelists, writing in the post-Second World War era, Maxwell Geismar observes: "The best new writers of today can hardly derive much sustenance from" the "literary efflorescence of the Twenties." (1958:15) The function of the novel was claimed to have been taken over by sociology. The novel was pronounced dead or deathly-ill. Referring to the cultural impoverishment in this period and the consequent death of the novel, Lionel Trilling remarks: "It is not then unreasonable to suppose that we are at the close of a cultural cycle, that the historical circumstances which called forth the particular intellectual effort in which we once lived and moved and had our being is now at an end, and that the novel as part of that effort is as deciduous as the rest." (1969:88) William Barrett makes the same point when he says that "the present generation has produced a literature below the level of twenties and far below what should be expected of 150 million people living in the most prosperous country." (1969:61)

However, the fact is that in spite of all the banal horrors of their culture, and the gradual deadening of their capacity to feel outraged, there has probably been in the post-World War II period, as great a concentration of good American novels as in that mythic period of exile and return, following the First World War. Except Saul Bellow, no one of the current generation seems a Titan of the stature of Faulkner or Hemingway. However, the achievements of some of the leading post-Second World War novelists, such as Robert Penn Warren, Saul Bellow, James Baldwin, William Burroughs, J.D. Salinger, Norman Mailer, Ralph Ellison, William Styron, John Updike, John Barth, and Philip Roth are considerable enough to allay all rumours of the novel's untimely demise. These writers, no doubt, reflect in their works the despair, guilt, spiritual aridity, violence, and repression of the individual by the ubiquitous organisation and war machinery. However, their works display a strong concern with the alienation of man through the protagonists of their fiction, the protagonist often becoming a sensitized outsider—what the sociologists call a marginal man, a kind of *Schlemiel.* Exalted fictional treatment of the hero shows him experiencing the sin and guilt of fellow humans and the protagonist even sacrifices himself for their redemption or performs an exemplary spiritual passage for his own salvation.

II

Several movements gained prominence in the post-Second World War period, being basically reactions against the socio-cultural, economic, political and religious ethos of contemporary

America. These movements attempted to provide answers to man's predicament in a hostile, fragmented and absurd world.

Black Humour was one such movement which emerged in the contemporary American fiction. The concept of Black Humour was developed by Andre Breton out of the premises of surrealistic disgust with the entrenched value-system in the post-First World War period. Andre Breton believed that "through humour one's self could be protected against the limitations of human condition, physical and psychological as well as social." (Weber 1973:363) In his opinion, the trivial reality imprisoning man through logic, reason, and subjective emotion, could be transcended. Freed by humour, the self, which is culturally determined, man's dark, submerged, unconscious could express its metaphysical desires in the form of dream, fantasy and nonsense. Black Humour made serious subjects the butt of laughter. It laughed at disease, physical deformity, mental disorder, suffering, degeneration of men and institutions. It also laughed at death. Black Humourists like Thomas Pynchon, Joseph Heller and Bruce Jay Friedman undercut the importance of emotions and sentiments, besides denigrating any belief in the eternity of anything and wilfully and deliberately attacking the fundamental eternal values of love, kindness, sympathy for the victim, and the nobility and selflessness inherent in sacrifice. Terror at the possibility of nuclear war, diminishing of individual liberty by the encroachments of bureaucracy, horror of fragmentation and dehumanization of man in a society in which technology played a dominant role, gruesome political assassinations of Kennedy and King and the Vietnam disgrace only strengthened the attitude and thinking of the Black Humourists.

Another movement which made its presence felt at the end of the Fifties was led by the Beat Generation. It explored the possibility of restoring to man his lost dignity. The Beats condemned the whole gamut of Western socio-economic, political and intellectual traditions. They felt scandalised by the devastation caused by the Second World War and vociferously castigated the technological revolution because it had a baneful effect on the human sensibility. The technocratic culture brought about a mass society in which "the population grows passive, indifferent, and atomized; in which traditions, loyalties and associations become lax or dissolve entirely; in which coherent publics based on definite interests and opinions gradually fall apart, in which man becomes a consumer, himself mass-produced like the products, divisions and values that he absorbs." (Howe 1969:130) David McReynolds also emphatically highlights the evils of the technocratic revolution by referring to the contemporary man's loss of identity, his sense of being part of his family and the feeling of oneness with the community:

> Cultural patterns are eroded by a system of mass production and mass communication in which we all become like one another, speaking the same language, wearing the same clothes, reading the same magazines. But instead of creating a sense of community, this only creates a crowd of faceless and anonymous men.
>
> How is man to know who he is today? By what does he identify? Not by a relationship to the soil on which he was born—for we have left the land for the city, where we flit like hurried vagrants from one apartment to another. Nor can a person find his identity in the family—for that institution is breaking down. This is the society of the mass. . . The individual is never able to feel that he is an important part of some meaningful whole. Our hearts ache with loneliness but we do not know how to talk to one another. (203-4)

John Clellon Holmes, a prominent spokesman of the Beats, contended that besieged by an inhuman world, the Beat Generation could consider the question only in personal terms knowing that "the only answer it can accept can come out of the dark night of the individual soul." (1960:18) The Beat Generation, thus, insisted on the spontaneous, the improvised as the guiding factors of human existence, in addition to advocating sensuality, naturalness, contempt for censorship, sense of holiness, and openness.

The vision of cosmos being meaningless, hostile and chaotic, society being formless and fluid, without the comforting assurances of stability left man helpless and bereft of a sense of purpose. Deprived of the religious support and political illusions, man felt bewildered and lost in an alien and frightening universe. This intellectual and spiritual crisis made the writers of the Fifties and Sixties turn to the philosophical expositions of Heidegger, Sartre and Camus. These thinkers viewed modern man's predicament in existential terms, considering the plight of man as arising out of absurdity and meaninglessness. Heidegger celebrates man's faculty of consciousness through which man alone "exists" whereas "Rocks are, but they do not exist. Trees are, but they do not exist."(1975:272) He believes that the absurdity of the universe may be transcended through "consciousness." Sartre finds hope for man in the absurd universe because man is free to choose. Through freedom of choice man may choose to be "nothing" like a "table" or may choose "to reach above the stars." (Kaufmann 1975:47) However, it was Albert Camus whose influence on the modern writers was the greatest. Camus also believes that though consciousness of the "absurd" situation makes man a tragic figure, but simultaneously it becomes a source of happiness, since "There is no fate that cannot be surmounted by scorn." (1975:109) Cursed with the torture of rolling the rock up the mountain and finding it rolling down again, Sisyphus displays a noble and defiant struggle against his fate:

> one sees merely the whole effort of a body straining to raise the huge stone, to roll it and push it up a slope a hundred times over; one sees the face screwed up, the cheek tight against the stone, the shoulder bracing the clay-covered mass, the foot wedging it, the fresh start with arms outstretched, the wholly human security of two earth-clotted hands. At the very end of his long effort measured by skyless space and time without depth, the purpose is achieved. Then Sisyphus watches the stone rush down in a few moments towards that lower world whence he will have to push it up again towards the summit. He goes back down to the plain . . . I see that man going back with a heavy yet measured step towards the torment of which he will never know the end. That hour like a breathing-space which returns as surely as his suffering, that is the hour of *consciousness*. At each of those moments when he leaves the heights and gradually sinks towards the lairs of the gods, he is superior to his fate. He is stronger than his rock. (108-9, italics mine)

Out of this hopeless situation in which Sisyphus finds himself comes joy as he recognizes the absurdity of the situation, defies his fate, and transcends a meaningless existential predicament. Camus compares the modern man to Sisyphus because both are involved in exhausting, monotonous, and apparently unending tasks. He outlines the helplessness of the modern man when he writes that in a universe which is without "illusions and lights, man feels an alien, a stranger. His exile is without remedy since he is deprived of the memory of a lost home or the hope of a promised land. This divorce between man and his life,. the actor and his setting, is properly the feeling of absurdity." (13) However, Camus does not believe that man confronted with the horror of absurdity, should accept defeat. Instead, he exhorts man to rebel like Sisyphus did and find meaning and purpose through rebellion.

The Absurd movement influenced the contemporary writers of fiction. Charles B. Harris (1971:iv) asserts that Sixties can appropriately be termed as the Decade of the Absurd. David D. Galloway regards J.D. Salinger, John Updike, William Styron and Saul Bellow as novelists of the Absurd who share a vision of the spiritual sterility and loneliness of the modern environment strikingly similar to the absurd universe which Camus described in *The Myth of Sisyphus*. These novelists further share with Camus the belief that man must oppose this universe, even though his demands for order and meaning will make him absurd. Galloway traces more similarities between these authors and Camus: "Like Camus, these authors reject nihilism and orthodoxy, and like Camus, too, they end by affirming the humanity of man." (1981:15) The absurd hero is a rebel against the reality which is constituted by the meaninglessness of life. Through his rebellion, the absurd hero generates values to replace those which were lost when the sacred traditions disappeared in the secular societies of the West.

In *Rabbit Run*, John Updike makes a specific and detailed analysis of the spiritual shallowness of his age. Harry (Rabbit) Angstrom rebels against the wasteland in which he is born and becomes an absurd hero by consistently opposing the reality he encounters. He finds that everything in his world is in a flux, but his intention is to impose order and value on that flux. In Updike's *The Centaur*, George Caldwell's experiences are almost wholly psychological, but like those of Rabbit's, they constitute a crucial rebellion against the meaninglessness of life. Styron's Cass Kinsolving in *Set This House on Fire* eventually learns the significance of other human beings in society. Through the new humility and love he comes to acquire for mankind, he becomes a social reformer. While ministering to his diseased friend, Michele, Cass concludes that hell is "*not giving.*" Bellow subscribed to Simone Weil's belief that to believe in the existence of human beings as such is "love." Bellow's emphasis is on the manifestation of love: either his heroes's great concern is to learn how to love or to find an environment in which love could be constructively and articulately expressed. Augie March in *The Adventures of Augie March* and Henderson in *Henderson the Rain King* embark on the quest for love.

Ostensibly, the most important developments in contemporary American fiction are represented by those writers who have grappled with the meaningless and with great integrity have suggested paths through the modern wasteland, though not being always able to chart those paths with complete precision. Recognising the discontinuity of much of the modern experience, these writers nonetheless have shown man's plight in terms of a continuous humanistic tradition. Without succumbing to despair, these artists express despair. They question and deny the validity of traditional consolations, simultaneously upholding the traditions of the human spirit. Despite its well known and often deprecated obsession with the self, modern fiction, on the whole, is not socially irresponsible. Instead, it insists upon a more valid relationship of man with society. Even though the novels of the Black Humourists, the Beat Generation and the novelists of the Absurd presented premises which could not be accepted in their entirety, yet their protagonists sought to safeguard, and attain the dignity of the individual, in spite of being besieged by the forces of degeneration and dehumanization.

III

J.D. Salinger's reaction to the contemporary numbness and exhaustion of beliefs is more positive. His protagonists, too, find themselves in a world full of squalor. In the fictional cosmos of J.D. Salinger, things like sham intellectualism and vain exhibitionism, chic shallowness and superficiality, cultural and spiritual philistinism, jealous aggressiveness and smugness constitute challenges for his protagonists. False values, self-aggrandising and self-advertising businessmen, betrayals in matrimony and friendship, senseless cruelty of war, pervading ego, perverted freaks (homosexuals) and rampant hypocrisy complete the picture of human demonism in a dystopian world. Salinger's protagonists feel shocked and disgusted, because they are sensitive, besides feeling out of place and out of sorts in the world they encounter. Suffering intensely, some of them feel alienated: Franny in *Franny and Zooey* has a nervous breakdown, which is symbolic of her alienation yet she does not finally forsake society and social responsibility. Religion and spirituality are not allowed to become retreats for escape from society and social responsibility, even though certain religious tenets are made use of to bring about the resurgence of the self. As Howard M. Harper, Jr., observes: "Salinger himself is critical of the spiritual exclusiveness of his characters; Franny's 'Jesus Prayers' for example, must be modified by Zooey's corollary that the concept of Christ has no real meaning outside of its human context. While Salinger does not deny the reality of the spiritual dimension of human life, he does question whether it should take precedence over responsibilities to other people." (1967:194)

Through a positive meaningful gesture, the Salinger heroes assert their sense of community and oneness with other human beings. Even adherence to family ties is maintained. For example, Holden Caulfield, in *The Catcher in the Rye*, has to choose between death and life, staying in society and running away from it, involvement with people and society and apathy towards them, and understanding the reality with a view to finding a solution to his predicament and discarding everything. He chooses life, a conscious acceptance of society, and involvement with people, even though he says, "Don't ever tell anybody anything. If you do, you start missing everybody." (Salinger 1958:220) Philip Roth rightly remarks: "The response of college students to the works of J.D. Salinger should indicate to us that perhaps he, more than anyone else, has not turned his back on the times, but instead has managed to put his finger on what is most significant in the struggle going on between the self (all selves, not just the writer's) and the culture." (1969:149) The basic predicament, that of the misfit hero, who is also a moral hero constitutes the genesis of Salinger's fictional world as the hero moves steadily forward towards pronouncements that stress human dignity, emphasize the importance of kindness and suggest the possibilities for individual redemption within the social space.

Salinger's fiction is, therefore, different from that of the Black Humourists whose protagonists sought to ward off their despair by transcending the trivial and disgusting reality and using their humour to protect their *selves* against the constraint of human condition. Salinger is unlike the Beat novelists whose characters, having felt isolated in the suffocating and decadent society escape from it and find fulfilment in destructive individualism. In fact, Salinger's attitude to perversions in sex and violence, practised by the Beat protagonists, is one of condemnation and rejection. Stradlater, one of the characters in *The Catcher in the Rye*, is censured by the chief protagonist, Holden Caulfield, for his promiscuous sex with girls. For Holden promiscuous sex becomes something totally detestable. Homosexuals are condemned by him outright. Violence is disapproved, as Sgt. X in "For Esme—With Love and Squalor," mocks Clay, another character, for having killed a cat, while driving towards Valognes. Buddy's denunciation of the Beats and their ways is unequivocal and trenchant as he calls them, "middle aged hot-rodders who insist on zooming us to the moon, the Dharma Bums, the makers of cigarette filters for thinking men, the Beat and the sloppy and the Petulant, the chosen cultists, all the lofty experts who know so well what we should or shouldn't do with our poor little sex organs, all the bearded, proud, unlettered young men and unskilled guitarists and Zenkillers and incorporated aesthetic Teddy boys who look down their thoroughly unenlightened noses at this splendid planet where (please don't shut me up) Kilroy, Christ, and Shakespeare all stopped." (Salinger 1964c:76-77)

A kind of similarity between J.D. Salinger and the optimistic Absurdist novelists becomes well discernible. Both emphasize the value of consciousness and both entertain hope about man. But Salinger's characters do not rely upon existentialist redemption, as most of the absurd heroes do. Even though David D. Galloway brackets Salinger with other major writers of the Absurd, Salinger differs from them inasmuch as he does not explore the meaninglessness of the cosmos, nor are his protagonists threatened by a hostile and meaningless cosmos. On the other hand, the Salinger protagonists feel threatened by a debased and decadent society, and this fills them with despair and disgust. The hero of the early stories feels also endangered by the incidence of war. What adds dignity and grace to these protagonists is that they attempt to live with meaning and nobility in the name of a worthy goal. For Salinger love is called upon to overcome individualism and alienation. The Glass family, in the Glass stories like *Franny and Zooey*, *Raise High the Roof Beam Carpenters*; *and Seymour: An Introduction* and "Hapworth 16, 1924," cannot imagine existence without human contact and love. But for Salinger's protagonists this is love for mankind rather than for any one individual. Human inter-relationships become a sacred formulation for the fictional personages of Salinger, the only question being how best to accommodate the inevitable relationships.

Holden Caulfield feels sorry over the absence of everybody towards the end of the novel—even those who shocked, disgusted and tormented him. Eloise, in "Uncle Wiggily in Connecticut," becomes aware of her degeneration, and makes a gesture of love towards her neglected and ill-treated daughter, Ramona. Ginnie Mannox in "Just before the War with the Eskimos" decides to keep the half chicken sandwich given to her by Franklin the clumsy-looking brother of her friend, Selena, as a token of his love and concern for her.

The riddle that Charles asks Sgt. X, in "For Esme—With Love and Squalor," could well be the riddle about Salinger's fiction:

Charles: "What did one wall say to the other wall?"
Sgt. X: "Meetcha at the corner?" (Salinger 1964b:100)

Sgt. X's answer is right: contact, human contact, its need and desirability and benefits arising out of it to men and society become dominant traits in the novels of Salinger. Lack of human inter-relationships can lead only to depression, alienation and even anomie. This all-important truth becomes the epicentre of Salinger's fiction, with assumption of social responsibility as one of its chief products.

Life and Works of J.D. Salinger

A study of the biography of any creative writer becomes a rewarding exercise. Events in his life, his personal relationships with family, friends, relatives and others, his religious, political and spiritual beliefs or the lack of these also provide scope for an interesting study of his works. The author's reactions to the contemporary sociological scenario, the ideas and values he cherishes, and also his life-style have, in one or the other manner, a bearing on his creative work. In case of J.D. Salinger, an interpretative study of his life becomes all the more essential because misconceptions about his mysterious and isolated life-style abound in literary circles.

Since 1953, Salinger has been living in a house on a dirt road in Cornish, New Hampshire, some distance away from the town. The house has a six-and-one-half-foot fence created around it. From 1961 onwards, his life has become that of a recluse, avoiding public gaze, not granting interviews or appointments and resenting the publication of any biographical article in any magazine. When he goes to the town, he speaks "Only the few words necessary to buy food or newspapers." (Skow 1961:84) Only a small group of friends have ever been inside his house. Outsiders, who attempted to contact him, had to send in notes or letters without getting any response. Small wonder, therefore, that Salinger came to be known as the Greta Garbo or the Howard Hughes (the elusive business magnate) of American letters, giving rise to literary gossip.

In spite of the inaccessibility surrounding Salinger and his reticence to talk about himself, details about his family and life have been gleaned. Jerome David Salinger was born in New York City on New Year's Day, 1919, to a Jewish father and a Scotch-Irish Christian mother. His father, Sol Salinger, was born in Cleveland,

Ohio and "is said to have been the son of a rabbi." (Havemann 1961:138) However, Sol did not ardently follow orthodox Judaism and became an importer of hams and cheeses. Prospering in this business, he became a wealthy and flourishing businessman and married "a gentile, Scotch-Irish Marie Jillich, who changed her name to Miriam to fit better into her husband's family." (French 1963:21)

Salinger was called Sonny in his childhood, and being a solemn, polite and quiet child, liked to take long walks by himself. He had no brothers and only one sister, Doris, who was eight years older than he. The young Salinger attended public schools in Manhattan's upper West Side, mostly securing B grades, with arithmetic becoming a tough proposition for him. His I.Q. test score remained an average 104. He was a tall, skinny boy whose deportment was sometimes poor. Here, the fact parallels Salinger's fiction. The Glass children in the Glass stories were also born in New York to a Jewish father, Less Glass and a Christian mother, Bessil Gallaghar. All the Glass brothers at times sound like Salinger—introspective, sensitive, hating what seems phoney and dabbling in mysticism. However, Salinger was not a Quiz kid, like Zooey and other Glass children were. At the age of eleven, Salinger learnt to play tennis well. At Camp Wigam in Harrison, Maine, he played tennis, made friends readily and was voted the most popular actor of 1930. His records show that "he went to a public school, P.S. 166, on West 89th Street." (Hoban 1987:38)

His parents felt worried about his studies and, therefore, enrolled him in Manhattan's highly rated McBurney School in 1932, when he was thirteen. However, he flunked out of this school a year later. (Skow 1961:88) Even though Salinger's childhood has never been discussed publicly, we get an impression of Salinger in adolescence from one of his friends who recalled that Salinger at this time "wanted to do unconventional things. For hours, no one in the family knew where he was or what he was doing; he just showed up for meals. He was a nice boy, but he was the kind of kid, who if you wanted to have a card game, wouldn't join in." (*Ibidem*)

At the age of fifteen, Sonny was sent to Valley Forge Military Academy in Pennsylvania in view of the problems he was facing in his studies and in keeping with the social status of his family. This particular Academy may be recognized as Pencey Prep, the school the chief protagonist, Holden Caulfield, attends in *The Catcher in the Rye*. Yet young Salinger was not like Holden Caulfield who despises material prosperity whereas Salinger used to talk of "grabbing the big loot as a Hollywood writer-producer." (*Ibidem*) His classmate Alton McCloskey who was first sergeant in Corporal Salinger's B. Company and who, after retirement, became a milk dealer, recalled "Crawling through the fence with Salinger after lights out to poach local beer taps," but he was "sure that Salinger never went A.W.O.L.," as Holden did, "and practised only accepted sorts of non-conformism." (*Ibidem*)

Salinger spent two years at Valley Forge and graduated in 1936, securing his only diploma. His career there, based on materials in his "201 file" has been discussed in detail by Frederick Pilsbury in the Philadelphia Bulletin. (1961:23-24) His final grades were: English 88; French 88; German 76; History 79; Dramatics 88. His I.Q. as recorded in the Valley Forge file was 115.

He did not spend his time at Valley Forge as a recluse and became a member of the Glee Club, the Aviation Club, the French Club, the Non-Commissioned Officers' Club, and Mask and Spur (a dramatic organization), besides working as the literary editor of the academy year-book, *Crossed Sabres*. It is not known how much he contributed to this year-book anonymously, but he did sign a three stanza magnificent floral tribute to the academy. The tribute has since been set to music and is sung by the cadets at their Last Parade before graduation. It runs thus:

Hide not thy tears this last day
Your sorrow has no shame;
To march no more midst lines of gray;
No longer play the game,
Four years have passed in joyful ways—
Wouldst stay these old times dear?
Then cherish now these fleeting days,
The few while you are here.

The last parade; our hearts sink low:

Before us we survey—
Cadets to be, where we are now
And soon will come their day;
Though distant now, yet not so far,
Their years are but a few.
Aye, soon they'll know why misty are
Our eyes at last review.

The lights are dimmed, the bugle sounds
The notes we'll ne'er forget.
And now a group of smiling lads;
We part with much regret.
Goodbyes are said; we march ahead,
Success we go to find.
Our forms are gone from Valley Forge;
Our hearts are left behind. (Skow 1962:12)

Some of Salinger's friends felt embarrassed by the poem because of its immature style. They even denied that Salinger had written these lyrics. However, in the Valley Forge yearbook, Salinger is listed as the author.

The early stories of Salinger, who had come to be called "Jerry," were written in the beam of his flashlight which was hidden from the Valley Forge duty-officer, by tenting a blanket over it.

II

Salinger attended several colleges, but did not obtain any degree after graduating. "In 1937, he was at New York University briefly, before embarking for Bydgoszcz, Poland, with his father." (Hoban 1987:39) In a 1944 issue of *Story*, Salinger wrote: "I was supposed to apprentice myself to the Polish ham business," adding further, "They finally dragged me off to Bydgoszcz for a couple of months, where I slaughtered pigs, wagoned through the snow with the big slaughter-master. Came back to America and tried college for half a semester, but quit like a quitter." (Skow 1961:88) The college mentioned by Salinger here is Ursinus College, which was a co-educational institution, sponsored by the Evangelical and

Reformed Church at Collegeville, Pennsylvania, and not far from Valley Forge. While at this college, he wrote a humorous and critical column, "The Skipped Diploma" for the *Ursinus Weekly*, for nine weeks. He told Miss Shirlie Blaney in an interview that he quit the school for lack of interest in the middle of the year and returned to New York to join Whit Burnett's famous course in short story writing at Columbia University. (Blaney 1963:23) According to Ernest Havemann, Burnett did not form a good impression of Salinger who was a quiet boy, making no comments and showing interest only in play-writing. However, Salinger's first story, "The Young Folks" which he handed in towards the end of the semester was considered polished and suitable enough to be used in the *Story*, being brought out by Burnett as its editor. (French 1963:23)

For one year after the publication of this story, Salinger enjoyed no further successes. The year 1941 saw a "short, short story" getting published in the remunerative mass-circulation magazine, *Collier's*, and a "satire" in *Esquire*. His story "Slight Rebellion off Madison," with Holden Caulfield as the hero, was bought by *The New Yorker*, the magazine with which Salinger was later to get exclusively associated. *The New Yorker*, however, did not publish the story of a young protagonist who believes only in utopian possibilities without realizing the realities of a particular situation, because America had entered World War II, and most young Americans were joining military service.

Eppes also records that Salinger told her about his having worked as an entertainer on the Swedish liner *M.S. Kungsholm*, during 1941. (1981:233) Salinger's story, "A Young Girl with No Waist at All," published in 1947, confirms this fact. This particular story contains a reference to the *Kungsholm*'s visit to Havana on its last cruise, before being seized by the United States government for use as a troopship. It is likely that Salinger was aboard the *Kungsholm* during its last Caribbean cruise, most probably spending the day of the attack on Pearl Harbor at sea. The ship did not dock in the New York harbour until Monday, December 8, 1941, thus making this fact a true one.

Salinger was keen on joining the Armed Services, once the United States entered the war. He wrote to Colonel Milton G. Baker, who was at the time adjutant at Valley Forge Military Academy about his having been classified as 1-B due to a slight cardiac condition and enquiring about the type of defence work Salinger could undertake. Once the Selective Service standards were lowered, Salinger managed to get drafted in 1942.

Whit Burnett published a second short story of the author in September 1942 issue of *Story*. Along with the story, Burnett also published a letter announcing that Salinger was attending the Officers First Sergeants, and Instructors School of the Signal Corps. William Maxwell provides further information that during the first part of his military service, Salinger corrected papers in a ground school for aviation cadets, probably in Nashville, Tennessee. (French 1963:23) The novelist again wrote to Col. Baker from this place on June 2, 1943, soliciting the Colonel's support for his application for being transferred to Officers Candidate School (Pillsbury 1963:24), though being not very hopeful of getting accepted by the O.C.S. He was instead, transferred to the Air-Service Command in Dayton, Ohio. Maxwell reports that here Salinger wrote publicity releases and was again transferred to the Counter-Intelligence Corps in the Fall of 1943 (1963:24-25). In 1943, he was also corresponding with Eugene O'Neill's daughter, Oona (who later became Mrs. Charlie Chaplin) in Hollywood.

In the meantime, whenever Salinger got an opportunity, he continued to write. A short, short story of Salinger was published in *Collier's* in its December 12, 1942 issue. During the same year, a man's magazine, *Stag*, purchased his short story "Paula" which has never been published. (Davis 1963:25) The next year (1943), Salinger gained more prominence as an author, with the publication of "The Varioni Brothers," a story about a selfless young man victimized by his greedy brother. His stories had begun to find a ready market. The *Post* published some more of Salinger's stories. The last of these stories, "The Last Day of the Last Furlough," portrayed Holden Caulfield as one of the main characters who is mentioned in print for the first time. Towards the end of the year, "Once a Week Won't Kill you" appeared in the *Story*.

By 1944, Salinger was "stationed in Tiverton, Devonshire, training with a small counter-intelligence detachment of the 4th Infantry Division"—almost similar to the situation of Sergeant X, the tormented hero of "For Esme—with Love and Squalor," one of the best stories in the *Nine Stories* collection. "The author, like Sergeant X, passed the time listening to choir practice at a Methodist Church in Tiverton." (Skow 1961:88)

On June 6, five hours after the first assault forces hit Utah Beach, Salinger landed in Normandy with the 4th Infantry Division. He remained with the Division through the Battle of the Bulge and came to be known as an aloof, solitary soldier. His job was to track Gestapo agents by interrogating French civilians and German prisoners. Ernest Hemingway visited Salinger's regiment as a War correspondent and Salinger got an opportunity to meet him. Hemingway read some of Salinger's creative work and in appreciation, exclaimed "Jesus he has a helluva talent." (*Ibidem*) In order to demonstrate the merits of a German Luger, Hemingway shot the head off a chicken. This act of Hemingway disgusted the sensitive Salinger, who used this incident to highlight the mindless cruelty of Corporal Clay in the story, "For Esme—With Love and Squalor," in which Clay shoots down a black cat without any rhyme or reason. (French 1963:25) Implicitly, Salinger makes his great contemporary an object of ridicule in his writings, though unfavorable references to any other living writer are meticulously avoided. In 1947, Salinger came back to New York, "finished not only with the military but with a brief unsuccessful marriage to a French woman physician, purportedly a psychiatrist, whom he had wed in London in 1945 and divorced a year later." (Heymann 1975:26)

More of Salinger's stories were published in 1945 and during the same year he made his last contributions to *The Saturday Evening Post* and to *Story*, besides resuming contributions to *Esquire* and *Collier's*. The story "I'm Crazy," published in the Christmas issue of *Collier's* "marked the long delayed literary debut of Holden Caulfield who had been mentioned as missing in action in several wartime stories." (French 1963:26) Holden appeared again when Salinger made his debut in *The New Yorker* with the publication of the long deferred "Slight Rebellion off Madison."

He lived on Manhattan's upper East Side in Park Avenue "with his parents and spent his nights in Greenwich Village." (Heymann 1975:36) The young author was known to be a gentle and humorous person, who loved to argue about grammar and who made efforts to make his skinny body look stouter with bar bells. Buddhism had not yet become the vogue, but he studied Zen Buddhism in depth and suggested books on the subject to his girl friends, whom he cultivated with dexterous ease. These girls helped the novelist to create his fictional dialogues by providing raw-material through their conversations with the author.

According to William Maxwell, a publisher was prepared to publish an earlier novellette type version of *The Catcher in the Rye*. But Salinger was not satisfied and wanted to work on it still more. (1963:26) At this time, having given up the military service, the author was trying to support himself by writing for the "slicks." "A Young Girl with No Waist at All," got published in the May, 1947 issue of *Mademoiselle*; the story being a nostalgic attempt to recapture the innocence of the youth in the pre-war America. In the December issue of *Cosmopolitan*, "The Inverted Forest" got published as a complete novellette. It was Salinger's longest work prior to *The Catcher in the Rye*.

Throughout this period, Salinger had been trying to achieve recognition as a writer and it came to him in 1948 with the publication of "A Perfect Day for Bananafish," "Uncle Wiggily in Connecticut," and "Just Before the War with the Eskimos," in *The New Yorker*, which "reportedly awarded him a $30,000-a-year contract," (Hoban 1987:41)—a mark of distinction for any young creative writer. In the same year, two stories also appeared in other magazines: "A Girl I Knew" was published in *Good Housekeeping* and the story reflected recollections of the pre-war Vienna, earning Salinger for the first time, a place in Miss Foley's *Best American Short Stories* of the year. "Blue Melody" which was Salinger's version of the Bessie Smith legend, appeared in *Cosmopolitan*. *Woman's Home Campanion* bought an early story of the Glass family, "Ocean Full of Bowling Balls." However, the publisher refused to use the story in either that magazine or *Collier's*. It was finally withdrawn by Salinger.

The pace of his writing had slowed down by then. "The Laughing Man" appeared in *The New Yorker* and "Down at the Dinghy" in *Harper's*. In 1950 only one good story, "For Esme—With Love and Squalor" was published in *The New Yorker*. It was presumed that Salinger was intensely absorbed in working on the Holden Caulfield stories in order to make a novel out of them.

III

At this stage, Salinger had already initiated a process of gradual withdrawal from society. He shifted from New York city to Tarrytown, which was a famed Hudson River community, where Washington Irving had lived. From there, he moved to Westport Connecticut which was a fashionable ex-urbanite community. Here, he once visited a short-story class at Sarah Lawrence College. William Maxwell records Salinger's reaction: "I enjoyed the day, but it isn't something I'd ever want to do again." (1963:27) His short stories had already established him as a reputed writer and as a consequence the young writer became an eagerly sought after person at literary workshops. But he assiduously avoided these invitations, primarily for the reason that he found himself becoming "Oracular" and "labelling" all the writers he respected. Exhibitionism and being untrue to himself became despicable for Salinger.

On 21 January 1950, Salinger's wish to have one of his works made into a film got fulfilled. The Samuel Goldwyn studios made a film "My Foolish Heart" based upon "Uncle Wiggily in Connecticut." But the changes depicted in the movie version evoked disapproval both from *The New Yorker* and the author. Though he had ardently desired that his works be bought by Hollywood, the experience of having this story filmed became so shocking as to make Salinger consistently refuse to sell screen or television rights of any of his other works.

On July 16, 1951 *The Catcher in the Rye*, the outcome of ten years's hard labour, was published by Little Brown and Company. Certain parallels exist between the author's personal life and the novel. One of the fellow cadets at his military academy committed suicide by jumping out of a window, like James Castle, a character, does in *The Catcher in the Rye*. Another cadet was expelled from the academy who later got admitted to a West Coast mental institution. McBurney's files mention that "Salinger shared some interests with Holden. He managed the fencing team, acted in school plays (portraying women and worked on the school newspaper, *The McBurneian*)" (Hoban 1987: 38-39) The spectacular success of *The Catcher in the Rye* turned the author into a celebrity. Salinger felt embarrassed over his success as people, eager to meet him, became a real nuisance. He found it difficult to avoid interviews, advice and autograph hunters. Salinger felt disturbed by the big photograph of his face on the dust-jacket of the book. He requested the publishers to remove it and they complied with his wish from the third impression onwards. He began to receive a large number of letters from his readers. Although he told Eloise Perry Hazard that "many of the letters from the readers have been very nice . . . I feel tremendously relieved that the season for success for *The Catcher in the Rye* is nearly over. I enjoyed a small part of it, but most of it I found hectic and professionally and personally demoralizing." (French 1963:29) In order to escape publicity, the novelist left for Europe.

In 1952, Valley Forge Military Academy selected him as one of the three distinguished alumni of the year and invited him to attend a ceremony to receive the award. He being away in Mexico could not attend the ceremony. Even though he wrote personally to the Academy thanking them for the handsome award, the award made him feel somewhat uneasy. (Pilsbury 1961:23-24) When in March 1953, the paperback edition of *The Catcher in the Rye* was published, 1,250,000 of the novel were sold. (Gutwillig 1961:38) Salinger discovered on his return that the "season for success had not died down." Therefore, he further moved to Cornish, New Hampshire, where he bought a gambrel-roofed cottage located on a ninety-acre hillside tract, with no plumbing or furnace.

Soon after his shifting to New Hampshire, his second book, *Nine Stories* was published in April 1953. It is a collection of all that he wished to preserve of his early short stories. "He befriended the Windsor, Vermont, high-school students, attending their ball games, and spending time at their local hangouts, Nap's Lunch Harrington's Spa, and inviting them over for long evenings of music and Zen." (Hoban 1987:41) In November 1953, Salinger granted an interview to Shirlie Blaney, one of his young friends, which was to be published on the high school page of the local newspaper, then the Claremont, New Hampshire, *Daily Eagle*. But the interview was not published on the High School page; instead a "canny editor, who knew a scoop when he saw one, printed it prominently on the editorial page. Salinger never spoke to any of the kids again. He erected a high fence around his house." (*Ibidem*) In the same year at a cocktail party in Manchester, Vt., Salinger met Claire Douglas, who was an English-born Radcliffe student. "She was unimpeachably right-looking, extra-ordinarily pretty, not too categorically cashmere sweater and flannel skirt." (Skow 1961:89) Claire was attracted to the thirty-four-year-old author—an intense looking man—and came to visit him at Cornish several times. However, Claire broke off her affair with Salinger and married a young student from the Harvard Business School. Naturally, Salinger felt disturbed because he had been betrayed by Shirlie Blaney and jolted by Claire Douglas. In the aftermath of these bitter experiences, the author further withdrew into the shell of privacy, retaining contact only with a few intimate and trustworthy friends. The year 1954 is a blank in his life history.

Claire broke off her marriage after several months as abruptly as she had entered into it. She returned to Cornish and got married to Salinger at Barnard, Vermont on February 17, 1955. The novelist broke his literary silence with the publication of "Franny" (the first of the stories concerning the Glass family, which had engaged him for about ten years) in *The New Yorker*. Jack Skow observes, "His wedding present to his wife was 'Franny' whose heroine has Claire's looks, mannerisms and the sort of private salute that amuses the author—Claire's blue suitcase." (*Ibidem*) Salinger hosted a party to celebrate his marriage with Claire. His mother and sister (about whom not much is known except that the sister is a dress buyer at Bloomingdale's and has been divorced twice) attended the party. Claire's first husband was also present.

The Salingers were blessed with a daughter, on December 10, 1955, who was named Margaret Ann. At this time, Salinger began another of his withdrawals from society and started devoting himself mainly to the two families: his own and the fictional Glasses. A son was born on February 13, 1960, who was named Mathew. Corresponding to the real life family additions, the Glass family also expanded with the publication of "Raise High the Roof Beam, Carpenters," in November 1955 in *The New Yorker*. At this stage, Salinger devoted himself seriously to hard work, leading a secluded life. In order to attain creative excellence, Salinger "put in as many as fifteen or sixteen hours a day at his typewriter." (Elfin 1960:93)

During the Fifties decade, few people saw Salinger, but the

popularity of his works continued to grow. His fiction got translated into Italian, French, German, Dutch, Swedish, Norwegian, Danish, Japanese, Hebrew, Serbo-Croation, Czech, Finnish, and other languages. Even in Russia, his works became popular, where possession of a copy of *The Catcher in the Rye* became a status symbol, among discontented adolescents. (Salisbury 1962:4) A poll was conducted among American literature instructors in Southern California by Henry Dan Piper and the result put both Salinger and *The Catcher* at the top of the list of authors and works published since 1941 that had achieved the stature of modern classics. (1962:20) Even Faulkner praised *The Catcher* as the "best" book of "the present generation of writing," because it "expresses so completely" what Faulkner himself tried to communicate. Holden also exemplifies the tragedy of youth inasmuch as "When he attempted to enter the human race, there was no human race there." (Gwynn and Blotner 1959:244) Faulkner goes on to say that Holden's story was about an intelligent, very sensitive young man who in this day and time was an anachronism, was almost an obsolescence, trying to cope with a struggle with the present-day world which he was not fitted for. (246)

The author's popularity attained its zenith in September 1961, when "Franny" and "Zooey" got published in book form. Salinger had announced that he would write a thousand-word introduction but instead he wrote a few witty and misleading remarks on the dust-jacket. The book, *Franny and Zooey*, "almost immediately topped the *New York Times Book Review*'s list of bestsellers and remained there for six months." (French 1963:32) The novelist had mentioned on the dust-jacket of *Franny and Zooey* that he was busy writing, being indeed engaged in writing "his first really large body of fiction," (Skow 1961:89)—the Glass family saga—which was intended to be far longer than *The Catcher*. But Salinger published little since his marriage. On January 28, 1963, *Raise High the Roof Beam, Carpenters; and Seymour: An Introduction* (a collection of these two stories originally published in *The New Yorker* on November 19, 1955 and on June 6, 1959) was published by Little, Brown and Company.

Salinger had been struggling, during this period, with his saint hero, Seymour, who had now evolved into a fictional being, endowed with supersensory perception. Seymour had first appeared in 1948 in a short story, "A Perfect Day for Bananafish," depicting his suicide. In his later works, *Raise High the Roof Beam, Carpenters; and Seymour: An Introduction*, and "Hapworth 16, 1924," the author attempted to explain the real reasons behind Seymour's suicide by delineating some important aspects of the fictional personage's character, related to his boyhood and youth. There are similarities between Salinger and the Glasses. "Like Seymour, he has written haiku and used to be an expert pool player. Like various Glasses, he used to have a penchant for reading his stories to his friends or relatives, and his interest in Oriental religion sounds genuine enough." (Grunwald 1962:18)

Salinger's preoccupation with the fictional Glass family left him little time for his real family. Claire, his wife, felt neglected and got dissatisfied. In 1967 she sued Salinger for "divorce, charging that Salinger's indifference and refusal to communicate injure[d her] health and endanger[ed her] reason." (Hoban 1987:41) Salinger did not contest the charge and they were divorced.

Salinger continued to write after his divorce in 1967, but did not publish. In an interview to C. David Heymann in 1975, Salinger told him, "I'm writing all right, but I'm writing for myself—not for publication." (Heymann 1975:42) Elaborating why he did not want to publish, the novelist said, "There's a delectable peace in not publishing. Publishing is a massive invasion of my privacy. I love to write. I write all the time. But I write just for myself and my own pleasure, not for anyone else's." (*Ibidem*) (See Betty Eppes, 1981. *Paris Review*, 23:8:238. Salinger reiterated to Eppes that he was still writing though not publishing. See also Phoebe Hoban, "The Salinger File," *New York*, 15 June 1987:38. Hoban writes: "According to some sources, he [Salinger] has two manuscripts locked in a safe and has submitted at least one work to *The New Yorker* within the last six years.)

IV

Salinger's silence and self-imposed seclusion continue. As he shares several traits of his personality with his protagonists, his living in isolation becomes discordant with the vision which his novels reflect. The only logical explanation for this seemingly paradoxical behaviour on the part of the author lies in the nasty experiences he underwent. Earlier, Shirlie Blaney had betrayed his trust and then Betty Eppes repeated the betrayal. She succeeded in interviewing Salinger in a deceitful manner on the strength of being a novelist herself. She later acted as a journalist, and syndicated the interview in a number of newspapers.

This treacherous act hurt the author's mind considerably. The interview with Eppes clearly reveals that Salinger, though living away from people,. continues to be a sincere, compassionate and humane individual with healthy views on different issues, and observing values which several of his protagonists cherish in the fictional world. When Eppes asked him as to why he had granted the interview to her if he was such a private person, the novelist's response was: "'You write. I write.' He had come as one writer to another." (Eppes 1981:234) Talking about giving autographs, Salinger told Eppes never to sign her name for anyone else. "It was alright," he said, "for actors and actresses to sign their names, because all they had to give were their faces and names. But it was different with writers. They had their work to give. Therefore, it was cheap to give autographs." (*Ibidem*) When Eppes said that the Constitution "seemed to have been written by men for men and that it may not have been intended for women," Salinger responded by saying, "Don't you accept that! Don't ever listen to that. Who says you don't have a right to the American Dream, who says? That's frightful. Awful! Don't you accept that. The American Dream is for all Americans. Women are American too. It is for you too. Proceed. Claim if you want it." (*Ibidem*:236)

The following incident speaks volumes about Salinger's personality and thinking. Eppes records in her interview that "I don't know if it was frustration, or intimidation, or awe, or what—tears began to roll down my face. . . . God, it was embarrassing! And I couldn't wipe them away—I had this friggy pencil in one hand and I couldn't move the other arm because it had the tape recorder wedged in [hidden] under it. Salinger smiled sympathetically at this point; he reached across and wiped those tears off with a knuckle, and then wiped his knuckles on his jeans." (*Ibidem*)

Salinger's protracted silence has fuelled rumours and speculations. In 1981, *The New York Times Book Review* reported on a rumour that "Salinger was publishing under the name of William Wharton." (Phillips 1985:41) However, Wharton turned out to be a real author who also led a private life like Salinger does. Mark Phillips suggests that in 1970 and 1971, J.D. Salinger may have written two long pieces under the name Giles Weaver in a relatively unknown literary quarterly called *Phoenix*, and he makes the suggestion on the basis of circumstantial evidence. For example, the editor's daughter had corresponded with Salinger; Giles Weaver suffered from neurotic depression like Salinger did, and the name Giles Weaver was well in keeping with the novelist's liking for using meaningful names in his fiction: Giles standing for somebody concealing himself and Weaver for the maker of stories. Besides, Phillips finds similarity in the style and ideational content of "Further Notes from the Underground" (written by Giles Weaver for *Phoenix*) and Salinger's writings. Phillips says: "Anyone who has read *Nine Stories* will recognize Giles Weaver's attitude toward a child: 'Also I designed [writes Weaver] and built a good three-foot diameter overshot waterwheel with the not inconsiderable help of an eleven-year old engineering genius.'" Phillips goes on, "Anyone who has read *Raise High the Roof Beam, Carpenters: and Seymour, An Introduction* will recognize this stylistic maneuver: 'This here isn't meant to be a definitive analysis of our situation and if anybody pleases themselves to publish it as such I will be pleased to render unto them a knuckle sandwich right into the kisser not via the typewriter but with my fist, so to speak due to the fact of the matter—which is to say, I find bloodshed a form of communication.'" Phillips further writes "And anyone who has read *Franny and Zooey* will recognize the philosophy of this Weaver passage: 'But it is no matter. I live for neither my own benefit nor yours nor anyone else, other than God himself. And I am sure that God is pleased with the great magnanimity of my spirit on His Behalf, considering how difficult He is: when I put my head out the window of my top floor room to have a word with Him, He's not there. Later I find He was sitting in the middle of my room at the time—and said nothing.'" There are several other pointers that the Weaver and Salinger are the same person. For example, "Further Notes from the Underground" expresses "Salinger's Zen-

Christian philosophy, his fascination with death and suicide, his loathing of psychology." (*Ibidem*) Giles Weaver also writes in "Further Notes from the Underground," about his depression: "How weird my depressions can get. So driven am I at those times for cheerful contact with anyone that those persons I encounter in casual contact, say in the stores, are deluded by my friendly foolishness. They are totally ignorant, with a great healthy will to remain so, of my black hell of perhaps only an hour before and of the fact that within five minutes I will be out on the sidewalk eyeing passing trucks with lust for the liberating contact of their wheels and my body." (*Ibidem*)

Whatever the truth, it seems quite obvious that J.D. Salinger, the creative writer as well as the withdrawn aloof individual, continues to be an enigma over the nature of his seclusion. Possibly he may not be nourishing any serious grouse against humanity, but humans like Shirlie Blaney and Betty Eppes shook his belief in the honesty and sincerity of those who tried to reach him personally.

In spite of Salinger's known inaccessibility and lack of cooperation from him, Ian Hamilton succeeded in completing the novelist's biography, *J.D. Salinger: A Writing Life*, which was to be published by Random House in August 1986. (Field 1986:63-64) Hamilton took great pains to complete the biography. Having got $100,000 advance for the book from the publishers, Random House, he spent $50,000 on research. He contacted about 60 people who knew Salinger. Hamilton made trips to the schools where Salinger had studied and wrote to his former classmates. He consulted the *Time* archives and went through whatever information was available on Salinger. He went to the extent of interviewing Salinger's agent, Dorothy Olding, "unbeknownst to Salinger." But he could not make much of a dent in Salinger's armour. Then he stumbled on to a reference book that identified collections of Salinger's letters. The letters revealed a lot about the novelist as "Reading the letters was like talking to the young Salinger." (Hoban 1987:42) Hamilton included many of the more memorable quotations in the manuscript. By May 1986, sixty copies of the uncorrected proofs had been sent by the publishers to the reviewers. Olding obtained a copy of the proofs from a bookseller and passed it on to Salinger. The novelist reacted angrily to Hamilton's book. On May 30, Salinger's lawyers sent a letter to Random House asserting that Hamilton's quotations exceeded "fair use." In order to avoid a law suit, the publishers asked Hamilton to revise the book by substituting the direct quotations with paraphrases. Hamilton carried out the revision and the revised version of Salinger's biography was submitted to the novelist's lawyers in September 1986.

Salinger's response was in keeping with his known attitude. "In his October affidavit, Salinger complained: 'I refuse to believe that an author such as Hamilton, with a clever lawyer at his side, can rob me of [my] right by using the guts of what I wrote so many years ago, with a few cosmetic changes, to flesh out an otherwise lifeless and uninteresting biography.'" (*Ibidem*) However, the lower court permitted publication because Hamilton had "cut down the amount of direct quotation." (Dalbanco 1987:27) But Salinger won the case in the U.S. Court of Appeals which stopped publication of the biography on the ground that "the book's main interest depends on its revelations from letters that remain Salinger's property." (*Ibidem*) Random House, Hamilton's publishers, applied to the Supreme Court for a writ of certiorari, asking for three questions to be pondered:

(1) Is the decision of the Court of Appeals for the Second Circuit that the Copyright Act bars virtually any quotation at all from or any fair use of technically unpublished letters of the prominent subject of a biography, even when those letters have previously been publicly disseminated, consistent with this Court's ruling in *Harper and Row, Publishers* V. *National Enterprises*, 471 u.s. 539 (1985), the Copyright Act and the first Amendment to the United States Constitution.

(2) Did the Court of Appeals correctly resolve the question left open by this Court in *Harper and Row* as to what constitutes the taking of "expression" as opposed to use of ideas and facts under the Copyright Act?

(3) Is it consistent with the copyright clause of and the First Amendment to the United States Constitution for a prior restraint to be entered against publication of a scholarly biography because it contains brief quotations and paraphrases

from technically unpublished but publicly disseminated letters?

Even though the petition launched a fierce attack on the Appellate Court verdict arguing that it would prevent the writing of biographies altogether, the Supreme Court denied Random House's petition for certiorari on 5 October 1987. Consequently Hamilton published another book *In Search of Salinger* through Heinemann-Mandarin London in 1989.

Ian Hamilton confirms in the biography that Salinger has been writing, as there are people who have seen the unpublished body of work "but they are not prepared to say whether they've read it." (Field 1986:64) Therefore, the only consolation is that J.D. Salinger is still writing and some day a more fortunate posterity may enjoy the fruits of his labour in full, when the unpublished works may get published.

The Early Stories (1940-1948)

J. D. Salinger's early stories. published between 1940 and 1948 form the first phase of his creative career. His first published piece is "Musings of a Social Soph: The Skipped Diploma," in *Ursinus Weekly* (1938). brought out by Ursinus College, which Salinger briefly attended. The first short story. "The Young Folks" appeared in *Story* (1940) published by Whit and Hallie Burnett. They conducted a short story writing course which Salinger attended and completed. Most of the early stories deal, in a mechanical and over-ingenious way, with the superficial interests of the slick magazine readers of the time. These slick magazine stories became a source of embarrassment for the writer after he started contributing stories to *The New Yorker*. a high-brow magazine, with his "Slight Rebellion off Madison" in December 1946. The spectacular success of *The Catcher in the Rye* in 1951 made the novelist a celebrity and. consequently. he tried to suppress further publication of the popular formula stories. except four of them: "The Young Folks" (1940). "The Long Debut of Lois Taggett" (1942), "Once a Week Won't Kill You" (1944c) and "Elaine" (1945a). These were "too discomfitting for the widely circulated journals that specialized in tales of consoling escape," and were, therefore, published in *Story* which provided "an outlet for works too unconventional for the slick magazines." (French 1963:47)

The early stories provide a significant genesis of Salinger's concept of man in his fiction. These stories delineate the nature of the predicaments Salinger's major protagonists find themselves in. An emasculating fictional world is created in these stories. a world in which man finds the integrity of his personality and his dignity threatened. The stories raise several issues seminal to man's relation to his self and to society. What possible attitude can man adopt in a dystopian world? He may escape into the comforting unreality of movies or his own imaginative fantasies. By doing so, he remains a sensitive outsider and, as Ihab Hassan puts it, surrenders to the "Assertive Vulgarian" who "carries the burden of squalor, stands for all that is crude, venal, self-absorbed and sequacious." (1962: 140) Or, alternatively, man may choose to grapple with the forces of corruption while maintaining the integrity of his self and trying to find a viable solution to live meaningfully. The interplay between the "Responsive Outsider" and the "Assertive Vulgarian" defines "much that is most central to Salinger's fiction." (140)

The early stories gain further importance by providing sources for some of the later works and characters. The stories in which the two Caulfield brothers Vincent and Holden, appear are used by Salinger in the development of *The Catcher in the Rye*. The relationship of Babe Gladwaller to his sister Mattie (aged ten) in "Last Day of the Last Furlough," and "The Stranger," prefigures Holden-Phoebe relationship in *The Catcher in the Rye*. "Slight Rebellion off Madison" forms part of Sally Hayes-Holden and Carl Luce-Holden conversations in *The Catcher in the Rye*. "I'm Crazy" (1945d) contains two scenes: Holden's interview with his history teacher before leaving the preparatory school and his conversation with Phoebe (his younger sister) in her bedroom. Salinger uses these scenes in *The Catcher in the Rye*. The writer-artist, Joe Varioni of "The Varioni Brothers" (1943), figures again as Raymond Ford (the misfit hero) in "The Inverted Forest" (1947a), who in turn, finally appears as Seymour Glass in the Glass Stories: "A Perfect Day for Bananafish," *Raise High the Roof Beam, Carpenters; and Seymour: An Introduction* and "Hapworth 16, 1924."

The dystopian world portrayed in the stories is promiscuous, phoney and castrating. It is a world of chic parties where *femme fatales* practise seduction through lies to destroy innocence. Even the "terrace" (an open space) becomes symbolic of the underworld which is "dark" as in "The Young Folks" (1940). Sexual promiscuity reduces some of the inhabitants of the dystopian world to the animalistic level. In "Go See Eddie" (1940a) Bobby (brother) "grunts" and wears "pig-skin gloves" and Helen (his sister) "horse-laughs." These are external indications of their inner degeneration into animalistic sex. Furthermore. "the State inevitably becomes omnivorous and omnipotent," (Lundquist 1979:3) through the army and emasculates man. War becomes a source of dehumanization, cruelty, disruption, grief and loss in men's lives. The war stories, viz., "The Hang of It" (1941). "Personal Notes on an Infantryman" (1942a), "The Soft-Boiled Sergeant," (1944a), "Last Day of the Last Furlough" (1944b), "A Boy in France" (1945), "This Sandwich Has No Mayonnaise" (1945b). "The Stranger" (1945c), "A Girl I Knew" (1948), "Once a Week Won't Kill You" (1944c), exemplify this type of effect. Yet in this abhorrent world, forces other than war add to man's discomfiture. Says Paul Levine: "What is so horrifying is neither war's physical brutality. nor society's overt prejudices but rather the subtle dehumanization, the insidious loneliness, and the paralyzing lovelessness" (1962:108) that one sees in Salinger's post-war world.

In this dystopian world of the stories it is the material prosperity which gains ascendency over artistic pursuits and destroys the artist ("The Varioni Brothers," 1943). Eve plays an emasculating role as mistress ("The Inverted Forest," 1947) and as mother ("Elaine," 1945a). It is a false world with "fake clouds" on ceiling on Seventy-second street movie theatres in New York and phonies who call "the Lunts" (actors in "O Mistress Mine") "absolute angels." Banality and tiresome routine constitute the hallmarks of this world. ("Slight Rebellion off Madison," 1946) In this world, psychotic husbands "Smash a lit cigarette" into their wives' hands and "crush" their feet with golf clubs. ("The Long Debut of Lois Tagget," 1942) This world is populated by "successful guys. ("I'm Crazy," 1945d)

II

In these stories not all protagonists are conscious of, and concerned with self. In "The Young Folks," a story about a party hosted by Lucille Henderson, where chic gentry are invited to drink scotch and indulge in promiscuity, William Jameson Junior escapes seduction by the society girl, Edna Phillips, not because he is a morally aware person; it is through his highly nervous nature and his interest in watching Dottie Leggett, a small blonde. Lucille Henderson, the hostess, happens to glance in the direction of Edna Phillips who had been waiting and trying to catch the attention of some young man for about three hours. Lucille looks around and gazes at the "noisy young people she had invited to drink up her father's scotch." (26) Seeing William Jameson Junior, a highly nervous person, she introduces him to Edna. Edna is the prototype of the phonies who appear in Salinger's later works: Sally Hayes in *The Catcher in the Rye*, Muriel, and her mother, Mrs. Fedder in "A Perfect Day for Bananafish," the Matron of Honour in *Raise High the Roof Beam, Carpenters; and Seymour: An Introduction*. Jameson wants some scotch and Edna, on the pretext of getting him some, takes him to the terrace, saying, "I think . . . there's some stuff on the terrace. Some kind of junk, anyway. Not sure. We can try." (27) She tries to seduce him by rousing his jealousy as she refers to her escapades with Barry, a Princeton student, and by indulging in amorous talk. But Jameson tells her that he has to go because he has to write an essay and leaves Edna on this pretext. The terrace Edna leads Jameson to is inadequately lighted "For reading, sewing, mastering crossword puzzles." (27) Her conversation with Jameson makes her intention clear:

> "Just look at the sky," Edna said.
> "Yeah. I can hear somebody talkin' over there, can't you?"
> "Yes, you *ninny*."
> "Wuddaya mean, ninny?"
> "*Some* people," Edna said, "wanna be *alone*."
> "Oh. Yeah. I get it."
> "Not so *loud*. How would you like it if someone spoiled it for *you*?"
> "Yeah. Sure," Jameson said.
> "I think I'd kill somebody, wouldn't you?" (28)

However, Jameson does not respond to Edna's amorous designs and retreating into the house joins a group of admirers, surrounding the blonde. Bobby and Helen in "Go See Eddie" (1940a), have no self-consciousness, nor do they try to understand the surrounding reality. In this story, both the brother and the sister lead a promiscuous life. The brother is a selfish and crude individual. He tries to force his sister to go and meet Eddie Jackson, a play-director, for a role. Helen hates Eddie and refuses to obey him. He feels infuriated and even uses violence to bring Helen round. He scolds her for her several affairs, but himself is carrying on with a married woman. Having regressed to animality, Salinger suggests, they will only continue to hit, hurt and deceive each other. An unselfconscious Bobby comments on his sister's degeneration: "You used to be a swell kid," (Salinger 1940a:123) but to no avail.

"Elaine" (1945a) is a story about three escapists: Mrs. Evelyn Cooney, a widow, her daughter Elaine and her husband's mother, Mrs. Hoover. All three of them are compulsive movie-goers. Elaine is an extremely beautiful moron who takes nine and a half years to get through grammar school and yet has no idea of what it is in girls that interests boys. She comes into contact with Teddy Schmidt, who after taking her out just once, marries her. But the marriage is shattered because of Mrs. Cooney. Elaine is a character who has no realization of her predicament caused by her escapist, inveterate movie-goer but domineering mother. Elaine runs away from her husband just because her mother wants her to. Having quarrelled with Teddy (Elaine's husband) and his mother, Mrs. Cooney orders Elaine, "C'mon, dolly," and she leaves her husband, and her marital home and follows her mother like a dumb sheep.

However, a majority of protagonists in the stories display moral awareness, besides awareness of their predicaments. "The Hang of It" (1941) is a story about a young soldier who has not yet been initiated into the army ethos. He keeps faltering during drills, and getting scolded by Sergeant Grogan. Bobby Pettit whom the army Sergeant, Grogan, finds to be "the *dumbest* . . . the *stoopidest* . . . the *clumsiest*, gink" knows that he is mentally out of tune with the bludgeoning ethos of the army and keeps repeating "I'll get the hang of it." (22)

"The Long Debut of Lois Taggett" (1942) portrays a self-centred Manhattan girl whose vanity cannot cope with the blow it receives when her psychotic first husband smashes a lit cigarette into her hand and crushes her foot with a golf club. She gets divorced from him and marries Carl Curfman who wears only white socks.

Lois turns into the same kind of cruel individual as Eloise in "Uncle Wiggily in Connecticut." She denies Carl the simple pleasures he enjoys and insists that he wear coloured socks. However, after her baby smothers in sleep, she realizes her mistake, changes her attitude towards Carl whom she had been torturing vindictively and allows him to wear his "White socks." Her self-realization and change are also analogous to the change of heart that Eloise undergoes.

"The Varioni Brothers" (1943) is a story about the consequences of capitulation to the lure of Mammon and ascendancy of material success over art and beauty. Sonny Varioni believes, "Success is what both of us need. . . . It'll bring in money." (76) Wielding tremendous influence on Joe, he compels his brother to write lyrics for his popular music and thwarts Joe's desire to write novels. He brushes aside Sarah's (Joe's student and friend) remonstrances who knows that Joe is a novelist and pleads with Sonny: "Let him go, Sonny. What do you care? You've got your break. You can get somebody else to write lyrics for you." (76) Professor Voorhees's remark to Sonny about Joe not being allowed to write novels is pertinent: "You're quite determined to burn out your brother's life?" (77) Joe Varioni has full realization that he is not protecting the integrity of his own self when he tells Sarah Daley Smith, his student-friend, "I haven't been writing." (76)

"Both Parties Concerned" (1944) is about Billy Vullmer and Ruth (Ruthie) who marry too young. They have problems on account of Billy's immaturity and the marriage nearly collapses. But Billy acquires self-consciousness and realizes that he should accept the marital responsibilities as a husband and father. So does Ruthie, who sees her mother in "her hair net again," and leaves her mother's house. She tells her husband that when he rang up, "Mother answered the phone, wearing her hair net. . . . It got me down. I mean when I saw her looking so funny in her hair net again, I knew I wouldn't be any good at home any more. I mean not any good at their home." (48) Though Ruthie is unable to explain what she means, the fact is that she is now a grown up married woman, and could no longer tolerate being treated as a child by her mother. Ruthie's mother would use a hair net during her young days, when Ruthie was a child. Seeing her old mother in a hair net again obviously implied that Ruthie was still being treated as a child.

"The Soft-Boiled Sergeant" (1944a) portrays the life and death of an ugly-looking but golden-hearted Sergeant Burke, possessing a conscious concern with life-furthering and life-preserving values. Burke's last advice to young Philly Burns, whom he helps in getting adjusted to the army life, is "Grow up and don't cut nobody's throat." (Salinger 1944a:85) During the bombing by the "Japs," three "buck privates" who had "just reported to the mess hall for K.P. lock theirselves in the big mess-hall refrigerator, thinking they was safe there.". (85) On learning this "Burke beat it out of the shelter" he himself was in "to get them guys out of the refrigerator." (85) Burke "got them guys out of the refrigerator, but he got gunned by a Zero on the way, and when he finally got them refrigerator doors open and told them kids to get the hell out of there, he give up for good." (85)

"Last Day of the Last Furlough" (1944b) is the story of Babe Gladwaller, a G.I. in the army. The story portrays the disturbed feelings of the soldier during his last day at home before being shipped overseas—possibly to his death. His addiction to ice-cold milk and chocolate cake, his preference for his childish sweetheart, Frances and his embarrassment while discussing adult matters seriously in adult company, symbolize his attempt to cling on to both physical and intellectual innocence. But he fully understands the real nature of war and, therefore, objects to his father eulogizing it. He says, "It's time we let the dead die in vain." (Salinger 1944b: 62) If wars are eulogized by those who participate in them and survive, "then future generations will always be doomed to future Hitlers." (62)

In "A Boy in France" (1945), Babe Gladwaller is shown on the battlefield as worn-out and tired, looking for a foxhole in which to spend the night. The story focuses on the dehumanization war brings about in those who participate in it. This realization of his predicament makes Babe worn out and listless. He attempts to overcome his despair by losing himself in memories and reading his sister, Mattie's letter, for "the thirty-oddth time." Vincent Caulfield in "This Sandwich Has No Mayonnaise" (1945b) is more than aware of the destructiveness and cruelty of war and world's coarse indifference to his grief caused by the loss of his brother, Holden Caulfield, who is reported missing in action in the Pacific.

"The Stranger" (1945c) is again a story about Babe Gladwaller, his friend and colleague in the Army, Vincent Caulfield and his young sister Mattie. Vincent has been killed in war and Babe visits Vincent's erstwhile girl friend (who is now married and is called Mrs. Polk) to tell her about Vincent's death and give her the poem Vincent had written about her. Babe is keen to deglorify Vincent's death and, therefore, tells her plainly how absurd, meaningless and unromantic his death was. The story emphasizes the callous attitude of the civilian world towards the rigour and the losses the soldiers have to undergo in times of war. Babe Gladwaller, on his way back from Vincent's girl friend's house intensely realizes that while the soldiers keep on getting killed in wars, tall blonde girls will continue to walk "zippily along," and a "fat apartment-house doorman" will continue to walk the "wire-haired" dog, "on this street everyday." (Salinger 1945c:77)

"I'm Crazy" (1945d) and "Slight Rebellion off Madison" (1946) are the stories which outline Holden Caulfield's conscious disgust with the contemporary phoney world. Holden's question to Sally Hayes speaks of his disgust: "Sally, did you ever get fed up? I mean did you ever get scared that everything was goona go lousy unless you did something?" (Salinger 1946: 76) Holden's despair becomes further clear in the question put to his friend Carl Luce: "Hey, Carl . . . You're one of these intellectual guys. Tell me something. Supposing you were fed up. Supposing you wanted to quit school and everything and get the hell out of New York. What would you do?" (78) Holden ends up with an office job in the first story and stifles the authenticity of his individual self. Besides, he knows that he is going to be one of those "successful guys." In "Slight Rebellion off Madison," Holden expresses his revulsion against the system of education, as it creates phonies and promotes the acquisitive culture of contemporary America.

Raymond Ford, in "The Inverted Forest" (1947a), is the prototype of Seymour Glass who, finding the twentieth century West as the "wasteland," discovers the "nice world" in the mind and begins to live in the imaginative world of poetry. Ford leaves his first wife, Corinne, who is honest and sincere. He elopes with Mary

Gates Croft (Bunny) who symbolizes contemporary American society: a corrupt, acquisitive, loveless world with false values, and false gods. Like Ford's mother, who is a torturer, Bunny invents "the very kind of physical punishments and 'wasteland' art that tortures the sensitive soul of the poet and forces him to escape back into the world of his imagination." (French 1963:73)

"A Young Girl in 1941 with No Waist at All" (1947), published in the fashionable *Mademoiselle* also, like "The Long Debut of Lois Taggett," (1942) becomes the precursor of "Uncle Wiggily in Connecticut," published in *The New Yorker* in March 1948. As Warren French rightly observes, "'A Young Girl . . .' also deals with 'the last minutes' of girlhood—those that the dejected Eloise, in the more famous story, had spent with the whimsical Walt." (77) Like Elaine in "Elaine," Barbara is unaware of what boys mean while talking to a grown up girl, but unlike Elaine, comes to understand the significance of it. Ray Kinsella, a member of the entertainment committee of the Caribbean Cruise-ship on which she is travelling with her would-be mother-in-law, proposes to her. Soon after his proposal, she declares to her travelling companion that she does not want to marry at all. She has become aware of her self and guards it by taking a decision.

"Blue Melody" (1948a) based on the accounts of the tragic end of Bessie Smith—the famous Black blues singer—is the story of a youth's awakening to the "phoniness" of the world. Fictional heroine Lisa Jones, a Negro blues singer, suffers from appendicitis during a picnic, and dies because the Southern White hospitals to which she is taken will not admit her. With her dies the world of Rudford who loves her. Rudford's consciousness of the squalor is intense. Years later, his unwillingness to play Lisa's rare recordings because the record is "terribly scratchy" indicates his maturity as he considers bringing back the bitter recollections of his youth a futile exercise.

III

Bobby and Helen completely capitulate to the animal world. When Helen asserts that she loves Phil, who is "a grand person," Bobby retorts: "You and your god damn grand persons. You know more god damn grand persons. The guy from Cleveland. What the hell was his name? Bothwell. Harry Bothwell. And how 'bout that blond kid used to sing at Bill Cassidy's? Two of the god-damndest grandest persons you ever met." (Salinger 1940a:123) She protests that "this is the real thing," and yet soon after Bobby leaves, she rings up Phil (Mr. Stone), and angrily snaps her affair with him because his wife talked about it to her brother. The irony of the situation becomes clear from the hints in the story that Bobby himself is having an affair with Phil's wife. The depth of Helen's animality gets confirmed when, having finished with Phil, she rings up an old lover, Hanson, making clear the nature of their relationship in her words: "This is me. Us. We you *dog*" (124) and bringing out her own bitchiness. Elaine escapes into the unreal world of movies under the influence of her mother and grandmother Mrs. Hoover, after having left her just-married husband. While her beautiful "gladioli corsage," which stands for her marriage, is withering away she exclaims ecstatically "Ooh, I like him," on learning that Henry Fonda is starring in the movie which she is being taken to see.

Bobby Pettit and Harry are bludgeoned by the army ethos into learning not to march "out of step." They are taught not to shoot way off their targets, not to drop their rifles while standing "at present arms" and keeping their rifles on the proper shoulder as commanded. Sergeant Burke who as an altruistic individual symbolizes generosity and kindness, and gets killed in the war. Babe Gladwaller learns from his friend Vincent Caulfield that Vincent's brother, Holden Caulfield, is missing in action on the Pacific and later comes to know about Vincent's own death during the action. In his despair, he is unwilling to enter into any relationship even though Vincent's erstwhile girlfriend tells him, "Call me sometime, will ya? Please. I'm in the book" (Salinger 1945c:77) Babe Gladwaller finds himself in the thick of despair when he is on the battlefield. The alienation and weariness brought about by war amongst soldiers is revealed when "He [Babe] passed by Hurkin [fellow soldier] who was sweatily digging a foxhole, and neither he nor Hurkin glanced with any interest at the other." (Salinger *Saturday Evening Post Stories* 1946:314) The atmosphere of bleak despair and gloom is evoked in the story by the use of symbolic imagery: time is "night" and the "cold," "wet" French sky has begun to darken, implying the bleakness and gloominess caused by the incidence of war. The blanket rolls used by the soldiers are "muddy" and a G.I.'s field jacket is "dirty." Even the afternoon has been "rotten." The floor of the foxhole Babe finds for spending the night in is "damp" where a "German had recently lain and bled and probably died." (315) Babe's own head is "filthy" and his shirt-pocket is "sweat-stained" and "mud-crumby." Babe's despair bursts out in "Oola-la" which he says aloud "half snickering, half-weeping." Vincent succumbs to despair over his brother, Holden Caulfield "missing in action that he cannot do his duty properly." (French 1963:65) The bitter feeling of helplessness of the protagonist, John, against war and its devouring cruelty comes out through the death of his girl friend, Leah, a Jew, at the hands of the Nazis. Besides, he feels disgusted with those Americans who remain unmoved by the knowledge of her torture and death. Salinger vividly highlights the despair of the protagonist by making him witness the usurpation of the civilian life by the army. When John enters his old sitting room where he had spent many tender evenings with Leah, he finds: "It had three single bunks in it, made up Army Style. . . . Officers' blouses were suspended on hangers everywhere." (Foley 1949:260)

There are protagonists like Joe Varioni who cherish a dream, but allow their dreams to be blown up by the narcissistic, acquisitive vulgarians, symbolized by his brother Sonny Varioni. The novel Joe Varioni is writing, is representative of his ideals. Salinger forecasts the fate of Joe's ideals by making him write his novel on "yellow paper, on lined paper, on crumpled paper, on torn paper" and at times "on the backs of envelopes, on the unused sides of college exam. papers, in the margins of railroad time-tables." (Salinger 1943:13)

"Once a Week Won't Kill You" (1944c) also records the sadness of the protagonist who enters the Army at the time of World War II. He is unable to get a promise from his phoney wife to take Aunt Rena to a movie once a week because the aunt ever since the loss of her husband, a second lieutenant in the Army in World War I, has been living in the make-believe world of movies. Holden Caulfield in "I'm Crazy" (1945d) is no doubt disgusted with the "phoniness" of his school, but he ends up with an office job, though knowing that he is not going to like it any better than the school he has been expelled from. He also succumbs to the corruption of contemporary American society—the creed of success and power. In "Slight Rebellion off Madison" (1946) again, Holden, finding himself caught in the vortex of an acquisitive and drab society, vehemently proposes a plan of escape to Sally Hayes. Having told Sally Hayes, "I don't get anything out of anything," and "I'm in a bad shape. I'm in a lousy shape," Holden suggests to her:

> How would you like to just beat it? Here's my idea. I'll borrow Fred Halsey's car and tomorrow morning we'll drive upto Massachusetts and Vermont and around there, see? It's beautiful. I mean it's wonderful up there, honest to God. We'll stay in these camps and stuff like that till my money runs out. I have a hundred and twelve dollars with me. Then when the money runs out, I'll get a job and we'll live somewhere with a brook and stuff. Know what I mean? Honest to God, Sally, we'll have a swell time. Then later on we'll get married or something. Wuddaya say? C'mon! Wuddaya say? C'mon! Let's do it, huh? (77)

Sally Hayes declines to collaborate. Holden ends up in a state of drunken despair and leaves Wadsworth Bar, with tears in his eyes. His "tears" suggest disillusionment of an idealist, cherishing certain ideals in a society full of corruption. Holden's alienation is reflected when the Piano player comes to the men's room and finding him sitting on the radiator asks him: "Why don't you go home, kid?" and Holden shakes his head and replies, "Not me. . . . Not me." (79) Barbara comes out of her drifting, indifferent state with her decision not to marry at all. Her decision makes her assume responsibility for herself, thus bidding adieu to girlhood. But conversely Raymond Ford, in spite of his being conscious of his predicament, is unable to "cope with the hard, insensitive world in which he must live." (Levine 1962:108) His elopement with Mary Gates Croft and leaving his wife Corinne are suggestive of his refusal to grow up. Bunny is as dictatorial as his mother. She is a shallow, adulterous and alcoholic monster, torturing Ford, into becoming an alcoholic wreck. Ford's dwelling in his imaginative world of beauty constitutes withdrawal from the harsh realities of the world and shows his incapacity to assume responsibilities. The symbols of Ford's submission to the vulgarian are the "renunciation of his glasses, the result of long devoted study, and his practice of eye-exercises to suit the taste of his [vulgar] mistress." (Hassan 1962:144)

IV

Some protagonists of the early stories do not exhibit any consciousness of their selves and their surroundings. Nor does the nature of their predicaments go home to their minds. The unregenerate remain in their debased world and the ignorant continue as immature and irresponsible persons who escape from the world into some unreal, illusory retreat. A majority of them become conscious and attain maturity. Yet, they voluntarily capitulate to evil and squalor or else find themselves overwhelmed by the forces of corruption, disruption and destruction. The incidence of war creates unnerving turbulence in the lives of people. Man feels marooned on the island of himself, afflicted with a growing sense of estrangement from his world and his kind, all this being again a consequence of war. The misfit hero finds himself unable to face reality, and a quiet mood, one almost of despair prevails in most of the stories.

In the early stories, Salinger's concept of man obviously remains in the formative stage, and the author seems to grope his way towards a positive concept in the later fiction. The novelist has not formulated a philosophy of existence for his protagonist which will enable him to understand reality, so that he may not only confront such a reality, but also live meaningfully with it.

The Catcher in the Rye

The novel *The Catcher in the Rye* was published on 16 July 1951 by Little Brown and Co. Salinger had been working on the novel for about ten years, while simultaneously he was writing other stories. Some of these stories were later collected and published as *Nine Stories* in 1953. The novel instantaneously became the focus of critical attention, as the *New York Times* reviewed it on Monday, 16, July 1951, the day of its publication. In fact, a review had appeared in the Sunday *Times*, the day before, and a rush of other reviews followed. "Through the later fifties, and onto the sixties, *Catcher* engaged academic critics: and still it does" (Ohmann 1976:15). In 1963, Warren French opined that critics had written more on *The Catcher in the Rye* than on any other contemporary novel, and in 1965 James E. Miller, Jr., (*ibidem*) claimed that Salinger had stirred more interest among the public and critics alike than any other writer since Fitzgerald and Hemingway.

The Catcher in the Rye is the story of a sixteen-year-old, Holden Caulfield. The point of view is the first person narrative. The sensitive, idealistic protagonist gets disgusted with the prevailing phoniness and stops applying himself to his studies. Consequently, he is expelled from his school Pencey Prep, as he had been from the three earlier schools. He spends the week-end in New York on his way to home and gets further depressed to witness moral corruption, perversions, hypocrisy, promiscuity and vulgarity. Bewildered and shocked, he goes to his former teacher, Antolini, for solace and guidance. But Antolini's act—which Holden suspects to be a homosexual gesture—when he was asleep, completely disillusions and alienates the young Holden who intends to flee to the West to live as a deaf mute in a cabin somewhere.

and work at a filling station. But he drops his plan of escape for the sake of his younger sister, Phoebe, who loves him intensely. While watching the carousel which Phoebe is riding, Holden gets an epiphany, making him realize the need to face life with all its lacunae and risks, and marking his growth into maturity.

In *The Catcher in the Rye*, Salinger enunciates his concept of man through young Holden Caulfield. The novel marks an advance in the evolution of Salinger's vision of man inasmuch as the central protagonist performs a journey from adolescence to manhood, innocence to awareness and from a mood of despair and renunciation to acceptance of society. Like the protagonists of the early stories, Holden also finds society unfit for living, but unlike his predecessors, after a temporary feeling of alienation, he accepts society.

He attacks the educational system which is geared to producing competent and successful Ossenburgers—undertakers who prosper through others' deaths. Holden also considers such people as glib hypocrites who talk "to Jesus all the time," (Salinger 1958: 20) but who pray for more deaths of other people. Christopher Brookman's assessment of the role of such schools (Pencey Prepp) coincides with that of Holden: "the type that such schools were created to produce was the bourgeois Christian gentleman, preferably with muscles" (1991:60)—"muscles" connoting power in several senses. He criticizes the religious fanaticism and narrow-mindedness of different sects, besides lambasting the concept of success which postulates only material prosperity. The increasing materialism of the American society in the post-Second World War Years is referred to by Michael Katz in his book *Class, Bureaucracy and School*. He observes: "I suspect that what the poor want for their children is affluence, status and a house in the suburbs, rather than community. a guitar and soul." (1971:139) Holden condemns sexual promiscuity and perversion that permeate the American society, in addition to castigating acquisitive values. The acquisitiveness has corroded human relationships and created a society where people are "crazy about cars"—the totems of status—and where they "worry if they get a little scratch on them, and they're always talking about how many miles they get to a gallon, and if they get a brand-new car already they start thinking about trading it in for one that's even newer." (136)

Philip Slater in his book *The Pursuit of Loneliness* underscores this characteristic of American culture when he says: "One goes abroad forewarned against exploitation by grasping foreigners, but nothing is done to prepare the returning traveller for the fanatical acquisitiveness of his compatriots. It is difficult to become accustomed to seeing people already weighted down with possessions acting as if every object they did not have were bread withheld from a hungry mouth." (1970:xii-xiii) Christopher Brookman compares Holden to Huck Finn: "Holden Caulfield, like Huck Finn, has become a mythic figure of adolescent protest in American Culture." (1991:57)

However, Holden's rebellion does not stop at cynicism and rejection of society. His solution to his predicament is neither escape into the orgy of sex, nor motiveless violence, nor perversion in the name of preserving his self. For Salinger, love is called upon to overcome individualism and alienation. Holden's love for his little sister, Phoebe, stops him from running away; his odyssey teaches him that reality consists of the beautiful and the sordid, the genuine and the phoney. The young protagonist learns to accept reality, while maintaining his dignity and integrity. His all-encompassing love makes him overcome his feelings of isolation. Salinger seems to assert that man should not abandon high moral ideals and his own dream even though feeling bogged down by sordidness and obscenity. For Salinger, an ideal man remains an integral part of society without capitulating to the evil surrounding him.

II

The Catcher in the Rye has generally been misinterpreted as a novel of escape and its protagonist viewed as alienated from society which he rejects. Hans Bungert believes that "the book deals with the estrangement of the individual from society," and that "Holden Caulfield is an outsider like Gatsby, Joe Christmas Thomas Sutpen." (Bungert 1963:177). For Brian Way Holden Caulfield is "a complete misfit" in society; his "despairing analysis does not permit even the stoical resistance of Camus, let alone the positive hope of Faulkner." (1963:192) Consequently, Holden ends up with a mental collapse. Bowden finds a dual desire in Holden who "wants to escape, yet wants to be a part of the perfect society, which he knows does not exist now." (1961:56) T. Morris Longstreth's opinion regarding the cause of Holden's loneliness and unusual attitude reflects an extreme and lop-sided assessment of the protagonist's character. He regards Holden's conduct as a "Nightmarish medley of loneliness, bravado, and supineness," and argues that Holden suffers from loneliness because "he has shut himself away from the normal activities of boy-hood, games, the outdoors, friendship" and finds him "preposterous, profane and pathetic beyond belief." (1963:12) Charles Child Walcut seems to have totally missed the actual thrust of Salinger's stance in the novel when he asserts that Salinger's *The Catcher in the Rye* fathered the Best Generation since its protagonist "hates schools, phonies, bores, movies, ugliness, and any sort of responsibility," and "depreciates everything." (1966:320) Holden's reluctance to adopt the profession of a lawyer—his father's profession—stems from his criticism of lawyers. He says: "Even if you did go around saving guys' lives and all, how would you know if you did it because you really *wanted* to save guys' lives, or you did it because what you *really* wanted to do was be a terrific lawyer, with everybody slapping you on the back and congratulating you in the court when the goddam trial was over, the reporters and everybody, the way it is in the dirty movies? How would you know you weren't being a phoney? The trouble is, you *wouldn't*." (179) But Walcut regards this argument as "infantile mechanism" with which "one could reject anything anybody had ever done for himself or the world." (1966:21) Holden not only "evades responsibility, but he rejects wisdom because he chooses to ignore the sound advice given to him by Antolini." (*Ibidem*:322) Thus, concludes Walcut, "Holden Caulfield's long weekend is an Odyssey, a Bloomsday of negation, emptiness, despair, loneliness, withdrawal." (*Ibidem*: 323) It is obvious that Walcut entertains an obsessive antipathy towards Holden's display of dynamic self-integrity. As Sanford Pinsker observes, "Holden demands nothing less than the highest standards of purity in motive, in execution, and perhaps most of all in triumph—or he rushes to the judgement that abject phoniness has yet again been at work." (1993:58)

The hero's proposal to Sally Hayes is considered indicative of his desire to escape from society. (Trownbridge 1966:686) and in his continuing identification with his dead younger brother, Allie (as well as his strong preoccupation with the equally idealistic James Castle, who committed suicide at Elkton Hills school), Holden can be interpreted as seeking, in an ultimate regression, the comfort of death itself. For Holden, it is assumed that this type of response can "be the only successful release from the agonizing complexities of a mutable and deceitful world." (Vanderbilt, 1963:272) Such opinions about the hero's thinking further illustrate the manner in which critics have blatantly misjudged Holden's respect and admiration for brave individuals like James Castle, besides his own abhorrence for a degenerate and rotten society. The protagonist's "catcher" and the "deaf-mute" fantasies are considered as "rooted in a single desire: a wish to escape from an adult world with which Holden feels that he cannot cope." (Seng 1961:207) Holden is accused of being "a rebel without a past, apparently, and without a cause." (Geismar 1958:198) Nothing could be farther from the truth. Holden's cause becomes abundantly clear from his strong denunciation of all that is phoney and false in society. According to Duane Edwards, Holden "has virtually no self-awareness. Furthermore, he has no intention of gaining self-awareness." (1977:554) Holden "withdraws from rather than faces the challenge of personal relationships" and refuses to "assume responsibility for his own actions." (*Ibidem*:554-55) It is believed that Holden withdraws not only from people but also Phoebe who is his saviour, because "significantly she isn't mentioned or referred to in the concluding chapter although characters peripheral to Holden's existence are." (*Ibidem*:559) This constitutes a gross misjudgment of the essential traits of Holden's personality. Hubert I. Cohen wrongly believes that "There is no indication that Holden has lastingly resolved his conflicts." (1966:363) Josephine Hendin asserts that "Holden rejects all the *rites de passage* that mark initiation into adult life—graduating from school, sexual involvement, faith that he can reach other side of the street or cross the line into adulthood." (1978:114) David D. Galloway, talking about Holden's role in terms of the Absurd, states: "while Holden's intention is absurd in its opposition to reality, the goal of his intention is to help innocent children avoid reality. His conclusion negates his premise insofar as it eliminates one of the two crucial terms of the absurd confrontation and offers no formula by which man can live in and with this world." (1981:208) Galloway, like others, ignores Holden's assertion concerning the desirability of universal love, need to cherish ideals, and act when necessary to protect one's integrity. Comparing Holden to Huckleberry Finn, Edgar Branch observes that "although each book is a devastating criticism of American society and voices a morality of love and humanity," (1963:87) they are still different because:

> Certainly if Huck's vision reveals both the limitations and promises of democracy—the hope and despair—Holden's indirect descent from Huck's, focusses on the despair. In the predatory waste-land of the city, Holden can foresee no future refuge or good. (*ibidem*:88)

Branch's assessment of Holden's situation being full of despair, does not take into account the evidence towards the end of the novel which clearly points to Holden's assumption of responsibility and his being "damn happy." Wanambisi's (1989) opinion that *The Catcher in the Rye* treats the theme of adolescence does not accord with Holden's mature perspectives on issues like consumerism, faulty educational system, mercinariness and pervasive hypocrisy.

III

Holden Caulfield is expelled from Pencey Prep for not taking his studies seriously. He fails in four subjects. He acts irresponsibly as the manager of the fencing meet with McBurney School when he loses "all the foils and equipment and stuff on the goddam subway," though it is not all his fault. It is obvious that Holden is apathetic towards his studies and irresponsible in his behaviour. The questions that need to be raised are: why is he so and does he continue to remain so?

The world of Pencey is nauseating to the sensitive, uncorrupted Holden. It is headed by a shrewd and calculating Dr. Thurmer. He includes steak in the dinner on Saturday night because "a lot of guys' parents came up to school on Sunday and old Thurmer probably figured everybody's mother would ask their darling boy what he had for dinner last night, and he'd say 'steak'" though the steaks were such "hard dry jobs that you could hardly even cut." (39) The school is full of phonies, and mean fellows. "For instance," as Holden says, "if you were having a bull session in somebody's room, and somebody wanted to come in, nobody let them in if they were some dopey, pimply guy. Everybody was always locking their door when somebody wanted to come in." (174) And also "there was this one pimply, boring guy, Robert Ackley, that wanted to get in. He kept trying to join, and they won't let him. Just because he was boring and pimply." (174) This school specializes in producing successful undertakers, like Ossenburgers, who donated large sums to the school and got school-wings named after them, besides getting opportunities to deliver hypocritical, self-righteous speeches to the students. The school also creates egocentrics like the middle-aged man who, on the Veterans' Day, visits the bathroom "to see if his initials" which he carved "in one of the can doors about ninety years ago," are "still there." (175)

Even a couple of teachers on the faculty, who are considered "nice," are in reality, phonies. For example, Mr. Spencer who is an old man and teaches History would "practically kill himself chuckling and smiling and all," (175) when Dr. Thurmer entered the class, supposedly incognito. The students at Pencey are no better. Robert Ackley has pimples besides rotten, mossy teeth and halitosis; Ward Stradlater, externally spruced up, is a secret slob since he never even keeps his razor clean. Stradlater is a narcissistic, unscrupulous and "sexy bastard" and Ackley is a "sort of nasty guy." (23) Earnest Morrow, his class-mate, is "the biggest bastard that ever went to Pencey, in the whole crumby history of the school. He was always going down the corridor, after he'd had a shower, snapping his soggy old wet towel at people's asses. That's exactly the kind of a guy he was." (158) All this fills Holden with disgust and, therefore, he decides not to devote himself to his studies. It is he who actually rejects Pencey rather than being expelled by the latter.

Through the hero's criticism and rejection of Pencey Prep, Salinger attacks the system of education which is geared solely to attaining material prosperity to the complete exclusion of human values which sustain a healthy society. This becomes clear from Holden's denunciation of the "Oral Expression" examination at Pencey. Explaining to his former teacher, Mr. Antolini, the reasons for his not doing well in this test, Holden says: "It's this course where each boy in class has to get up in class and make a speech. You know. Spontaneous and all. And if the boy digresses at all, you're supposed to yell 'Digression' at him as fast as you can. It just about drove me crazy. I got an *F* in it." (190) Holden goes on to explain, "That digression business got on my nerves. I don't know. The trouble with me is, I *like* it when somebody digresses. It's more interesting and all." When Antolini asks, "You don't care to have somebody stick to the point when he tells you something?" Holden answers:

> Oh sure! I like somebody to stick to the point and all. But I don't like them to stick *too* much to the point. I don't know. I guess I don't like when somebody sticks to the point *all* the time. The boys that got the best marks in Oral Expression were the ones that stuck to the point all the time—I admit it. But there was this one boy, Richard Kinsella. He didn't stick to the point too much, and they were always yelling 'Digression' at him. . . . For instance, he made this speech about this farm his father bought in Vermont. What he did was, Richard Kinsella, he'd *start* telling you all about that stuff—then all of a sudden, he'd start telling you about this letter his mother got from his uncle, and how his uncle got polio and all when he was forty-two-years-old, and how he wouldn't let anybody come to see him in the hospital because he didn't want anybody to see him with a brace on. It didn't have much to do with the farm—I admit it—but it was *nice*. It's nice when somebody tells you about their uncle. Especially when they start out telling you about their father's farm and then all of a sudden get more interested in their uncle. I mean it's dirty to keep yelling 'Digression!' (190-91)

Holden's disgust over "digressions" hurled at Richard Kinsella by his classmates constitutes a clear condemnation of the inhumanity inherent in the system of education in contemporary America.

Salinger traces the genesis of the inhuman violence and aggression afflicting American society like a malaise. Young children at school are infused with the spirit of fierce competitiveness which lets loose a rat-race for material success in society. The consequent dehumanization of the young in educational institutions leaves no scope for compassion or sympathy for the weak. In such a dehumanized set up, victory over the weak is glorified and eulogized. As the young hero stands watching "two teams [Saxon Hall and Pencey Prep] bashing each other all over the place," (6) he perceives the football game as an instrument of inculcating violence, which blunts the finer instincts. The protagonist's concept of the game is that it is a ritualization of aggression in society, favouring the strong and the victorious and running down the weak and the losers. Small wonder, that such a society produces Ossenburgers and puts them on a moral pedestal. Brookman rightly sums up Holden's attitude to the educational system in America: "Holden's commentaries on the value system of Pencey Prep lead him to conclude that the official vision of the school as a cooperative caring family is a mask for an actual ideology of intense competitive struggle between individual members and factions." (1991:61) It was actually because of this perception of games that Holden, subconsciously, became irresponsible as the manager of the fencing team and lost "the foils and equipment and stuff on the goddam subway." (7)

Pencey is the fourth school which Holden leaves. The previous schools were no better and made Holden feel out of place. Whooton School created vain exhibitionists and perverts like Carl Luce. Elkton Hills School proliferated with phonies and violence. At Elkton Hills, Sabile and his cronies tortured and killed James Castle, and got away with it without incurring punishment. The hero's revulsion against the educational system is summed up in his angry outburst to Sally Hayes:

> all you do at school is study, so that you can learn enough to be smart enough to be able to buy a goddam Cadillac some day, and you have to keep making believe you give a damn if the football team loses, and all you do is talk about girls and liquor and sex all day, and everybody sticks together in

> these dirty little goddam clicks. The guys that are on the basket ball team stick together, the Catholics stick together, the goddam intellectuals stick together, the guys that play bridge stick together. Even the guys that belong to the goddam Book-of-the-Month Club stick together. (137)

Holden draws a graphic picture of the society being created by the prevailing educational system:

> We'd have to go downstairs in elevators with suitcases and stuff. We'd have to phone up everybody and tell 'em goodbye and send them postcards from hotels and all. And I'd be working in some office, making a lot of dough, and riding to work in cabs and Madison Avenue buses, and reading newspapers, and playing bridge all the time, and going to the movies and seeing a lot of stupid shorts and coming attractions and newsreels. (139)

Holden's rejection of such a system of education is reflected in his intentionally failing in four out of five subjects.

The world of adults outside Pencey is worse. "Where the world of Holden's school was muted purgatory, the world of his New York hotel is an insistent Hell." (Baumbach 1965:62) At Edmont hotel the young hero witnesses a transvestite's feminine antics. Looking out of the window of his room, he sees in the opposite room a grey-haired, very distinguished-looking man do something unbelievable: "First he put his suitcase on the bed. Then he took out all these women's clothes, and put them on. Real women's clothes—silk stockings, high-heeled shoes, brassiere, and one of those corsets with the straps hanging down and all. Then he put on this very tight black evening dress. . . . Then he started walking up and down the room, taking these very small steps, the way a woman does, and smoking a cigarette and looking at himself in the mirror." (66)

He also sees a perverted couple squirting some liquid with their mouths at each other. Holden also meets three moronic girls in the lavender room of the hotel. Being shallow and ignorant, their only interest in life is to see movies and movie actors. Holden finds

Ernie, the virtuoso piano-player at the Ernie's night club, to be a snob and a phoney. In Holden's words, "he won't even talk to you unless you're a big shot or a celebrity or something" (85) though at the end of the performance, he "turned around on his stool and gave this very phoney, *humble* bow." (89) While sitting in this night club he becomes privy to promiscuity. Holden finds himself surrounded by "jerks." To his right, was sitting "this very Joe-Yale-looking guy in a flannel suit and one of those flitty-looking tattersall vests." (90) This fellow "had a terrific-looking girl with" him and "What he was doing, he was giving her a feel under the table, and at the same time, telling her all about some guy in his dorm that had eaten a whole bottle of aspirin and nearly committed suicide. His date kept saying to him, 'How horrible. . . . Don't, darling. Please, don't. Not here.'" (90)

His being manhandled and cheated by the pimp, Maurice, and the prostitute, Sonny, at the hotel further intensify Holden's disgust with society. Even with his girl-friend, Sally Hayes, the young hero feels disgusted because of latter's superficiality, and her inability to understand his predicament and sympathize with his mental state. All Sally is interested in is fashions, and showing off. Having said "Oh darling, I love you, too," in the same breath, she says to Holden, "Promise me you'll let your hair grow. Crew cuts are getting corny. And your hair's so lovely." (131) Besides, she is quite a phoney, as she has come out with Holden to see the movie, but begins to flirt with another acquaintance, George, whom she espies in the lobby of the theatre. Her insistence on going for skating is motivated by her desire to show off because she knows she would look nice in those "darling little skating skirts." But when Holden, who is feeling depressed tries to explain to her his predicament, all he gets from her in response is, "I don't know what you're even talking about." (136) His innocent girl-friend, Jane Gallaghar's perverted step-father, Cudahy, probably has sexual designs on her. Carl Luce, Holden's friend and former Student Advisor at Whooton School, is a snob and a suspected homosexual himself, though he was always telling the students about "flits and lesbians" and said that "half the married guys in the world were flits and didn't even know it." (149) As Students' Advisor at Whooton Luce used to give them "sex talks and all, late at night when there was a bunch of guys in his room," and "whenever he went to the can, he always left the goddam door open and *talked*." (149)

The bartender at the Wicker Bar, where Holden meets Luce, is also a big snob. He hardly talks to any other person than big shots. "If you *were* a big shot or a celebrity or something, then he was more nauseating. He'd go up to you and say, with this big charming smile, like he was helluva swell guy if you knew him, 'Well! How's Connecticut?' or 'How's Florida?'" (148) Jane Gallaghar's perverted father, Cudahy, her idiotic brawny, show off. boy friend, and "flitty" Carl Luce become nauseating for Holden.

The protagonist admires Mr. Antolini, his former school teacher at Elkton Hills, who shows sympathetic understanding of Holden's mental turbulence. Antolini tries to make Holden conscious of the flaw in his attitude towards society and remarks, "But I can very clearly see you dying nobly, one way or another, for some highly unworthy cause," (195) and quotes a psychoanalyst, Wilhelm Stekel's definition of an immature man: "The mark of the immature man is that he wants to die nobly for a cause, while the mark of the mature man is that he wants to live humbly for one." (195) Antolini also suggests to Holden, "I think one of these days . . . you're going to have to find out where you want to go. And then you've got to start going there. But immediately. You can't afford to lose a minute." (195) Antolini wants Holden to keep his priorities clear for achieving his goal and tells him that "you're not the first person who was ever confused and frightened and even sickened by human behaviour. You're by no means alone on that score, you'll be excited and *stimulated* to know. Many, many men have been just as troubled morally and spiritually as you are right now." (196) Importance of education is stressed by Antolini, as it is through education that Holden can better understand his aptitude and work his way towards his goal. But even Antolini disillusions the young hero and causes revulsion in him, as he ultimately gives the impression of being a homosexual. Holden describes what led to this impression of Antolini. He went off to sleep, having responded to Antolini's, "All right. Good Night, handsome," (198) with "G'night Sir. Thanks a lot." (198) Then, Holden says, "something happened. I don't even like to talk about it. But he does and says:

> I woke up all of a sudden. I don't know what time it was or anything. I felt something on my head, some guy's hand. Boy, it really scared hell out of me. What it was, it was Mr. Antolini's hand. What he was doing was, he was sitting on the floor right next to the couch, in the dark and all, and he was sort of petting me or patting me on the goddam head. Boy, I'll bet I jumped about a thousand feet. (198-99)

When Holden asks Antolini as to what he was doing, his answer is "Nothing! I'm simply sitting here, admiring," (199) and asks Holden to keep his "voice down." The young hero knows from past experience what Antolini was doing: "I know more damn perverts, at schools and all, than anybody you ever met, and they're always being perverty when *I'm* around." (199) "This image of a bleak moral climate which destroys the soul is not only the keynote of J.D Salinger's *The Catcher in the Rye* but of much that now seems representative of the general tone of American cultural commentary in the aftermath of World War Two, when the novel was conceived." (Rowe:1991)

IV

Holden's exposure to sham, pretence and social decadence results in a feeling of alienation and a longing for escape from such a society:

> I decided I'd never go home again and I'd never go to another school again. I decided I'd just see old Phoebe and sort of say good-bye to her and all, and give her back her Christmas dough, and then I'd start hitch-hiking my way out West. I figured I could get a job at a filling station somewhere, [there] putting gas and oil in people's cars. I didn't care what kind of a job it was though. Just so people didn't know me and I didn't know anybody. I thought what I'd do was, I'd pretend I was one of those deaf mutes. That way I wouldn't have to have any goddam stupid useless conversation with anybody. (205)

"With its wider hospitality to the values of rugged individuality, self-reliance and boundless freedom, the West has a deep mythic appeal," (Pinsker 1993:89) and Holden is not the only literary protagonist who longs for the West. Jack Burden, the brooding narrator of Robert Penn Warren's *All the King's Men* is also attracted to the West. (1946) But Holden's detailed plan remains only a charming fantasy. He does not implement it because he is incapable of such a recourse. He has all along been so involved with society, that he could not run away from it. His erasing the "Fuck Yous," his tightening the "skates" of a small girl in the park, his guiding the two young children into the museum to show them mummies and his concern for their having missed school, his appreciation of the "family"—parents and a child—that had just come out of a Church and his intense love for his younger sister, Phoebe, provide ample evidence of Holden's real disposition. His desire to be a "Catcher in the Rye," saving children from falling over the edge of the cliff is indicative of his concern with the security of children who, unprotected and unguided, may come to harm and does not connote, as claimed by Peter J. Seng, his wish to escape reality. Besides, Holden displays self-awareness when he remarks that "You can't never find a place that's nice and peaceful, because there isn't any." (210) The young hero awakens to his sense of responsibility when Phoebe insists on accompanying him in his escape. Phoebe meets him with her suitcase, containing her clothes, to go away with him. Holden gets a shock: "I almost fell over when she said that. I swear to God I did. I got sort of dizzy and I thought I was going to pass out or something." (212) Holden becomes very angry with Phoebe, and decisively tells her: "You're not *going*. Now shut up!" (213) In his anger he thinks, he "was going to smack her for a second or two." (213)

A glorious misperception of the reasons why Holden refuses to let Phoebe accompany him is contained in Susan K. Mitchell's argument when she, alluding to Holden's guilt for not taking Allie along for a picnic with his friend, holds that "in spite of his guilt over Allie, he commits the same guilt-inducing act with Phoebe as he refuses to allow her to accompany him on the new expedition." (1992:153) What Mitchell does not realize is that this time Holden is not going for fun; he is contemplating an uncharted flight to the unknown territory, full of uncertainties, and hardship, even danger. And somewhere in his mind, his own solution of escape is not really desirable. Therefore, he wants her to continue going to school. He wants her to act in the play at school. He is sarcastic with her: "I thought you were supposed to be in a play at school and all. I suppose you were supposed to be Benedict Arnold in that play and all." (213) Holden admits that he said "it very nasty." Phoebe began to cry and Holden says that "I was glad. All of a sudden I wanted her to cry till her eyes practically dropped out. I almost hated her. I think I hated her most because she wouldn't be in that play any more if she went away with me." (213) He tells her, "I'm not going away anywhere. I changed my mind. So stop crying and shut up . . . C'mon, now, I'll walk you back to school. C'mon, now. You'll be late," and reassures her, "I'm going home as soon as you go back to school." (214) Being conscious of social degeneration, he dismisses his plan for escape. He assumes responsibility for Phoebe because he does not want her to be exposed to the degeneration of a wayward life. Holden's ideal dream of becoming a "catcher" of children and protecting them gets realized in the rejection of his plan of escape and acting as Phoebe's guardian. Phoebe's riding the carousel also proves crucial in Holden's attaining maturity and facing the reality. All the children riding the carousel keep trying to catch the gold ring in the centre and so does Phoebe. Holden feels afraid lest Phoebe should "fall off the horse," but he does not "say anything or do anything." He decides that the "thing with kids is, if they want to grab for the gold ring, you have to let them do it, and not say anything. If they fall off, they fall off, but it's bad if you say anything to them." (218) His anxiety over Phoebe's attempts to catch the gold ring on the moving carousel gives way to the revelation that life with all its rigours, risks and obscenity needs to be faced with the typical American pragmatic spirit, without capitulating to the prevalent social corruption. It is this positive resolution of the protagonist's conflict which makes him incomparably happy. Pinsker supports this interpretation of the carousel scene when he says: "He cannot save her from all the risks, and joys, that, taken together, constitute life, nor is he any longer willing to try. Part of the sheer joy in the moment is a newly quiet acceptance of the human condition as it is, and must be." (1993:94)

His joy is reflected in his own words: "I felt so damn happy if you want to know the truth. I don't know why." (219) The tension arising out of the conflict between his desire to preserve the integrity of his self while grappling with a dystopian society ceases to afflict him any more. The young hero becomes finally convinced that it is possible to maintain one's dream even amidst the corruption of the world. No doubt, it is a difficult and painful exercise, but nothing less can lead to happiness. Nevertheless, the nervous strain Holden has undergone before the solution of his conflict takes its toll and he suffers a nervous breakdown. The protagonist's response to the psychiatrist's question, whether he is going to apply himself, is revealing. Significantly, he does not repudiate action since the emphasis in his answer is on "*do*," underscoring the importance of action and implying acceptance of society.

Holden's answer to his elder brother D.B.'s question as to how he looks upon his crisis constitutes another landmark in the protagonist's becoming mature. His awareness of corruption and obscenity in society no longer prevents him from cherishing universal love. He says: "About all I know is, I sort of *miss* everybody I told you about. Even old Stradlater and Ackley, for instance. I think I even miss that goddam Maurice. It's funny. Don't ever tell anybody anything. If you do, you start missing everybody." (220)

Even when Holden feels disgusted with the pervading squalor, he is able to recognise whatever is likable or admirable. He feels attracted by simplicity, innocence, love and sincerity. Several critics of the novel are mistaken in their stance that Holden hates everybody. Arguing that Holden escapes into the "illusion" of becoming a catcher in the rye, and, therefore, attains only "imperfect, tentative initiation," Isaac Sequeira maintains that "The people he [Holden] admires most are kids or adults influenced by kids." (1975:116) Sequeira goes on to list the names of Allie (Holden's dead younger brother), James Castle (a student who committed suicide at Elkton Hills), Phoebe, and the six-year-old boy walking behind his "uncaring parents" in a crowded New York street and singing Robert Burns's song "Comin' thru the Rye." However, the fact is that Holden does like several adults whom he finds to be sincere, affectionate, simple-hearted and straightforward. These people include: the dedicated, simple-looking Catholic nuns (120) at Grand Central Station, the quiet self-effacing but competent performer, the Kettle-drummer (143) at the orchestra in the stage show, the hatcheck girl (159) at Setan Hotel for her goodness and affectionate concern for him, and Jane Gallaghar for her innocence. (36) Of course, he also admires James Castle for his courage and dignity, as he prefers death to the ignominy of retracting his statement, his dead younger brother, Allie, for his affectionate understanding and tolerance, his younger sister Phoebe, for her selfless love towards him and Haris Macklin for being a "terrific whistler." Furthermore, Holden not only admires the six-year-old boy walking behind his parents, but also the "family." The young hero, referring to the weather, says that "it wasn't too nice for walking. But there was one nice thing. This family that you could tell just came out of some church were walking right in front of me—a father, a mother, and a little kid about six-years-old." (121)

All this conclusively establishes Holden's capacity to perceive the good, which in turn proves that his alienation is caused by the repulsive elements in society and not by his own thinking. Pinsker's observation supports this stance: "Holden has a fatal attraction for minor characters, not hot-shots, but those who follow their bents without compromise or apology. That the larger world misunderstands them is proof, if any were needed that they are authentic rather than phoney, innocent as opposed to corrupted." (1993:68)

One cannot agree with Mitchell that "the book lacks a genuine center—the center of the book [Holden] is actually phoney." (1992:156) It is in fact through Holden that Salinger holds forth the answer to man's sociological predicament which postulates a decent regard and love for others; moral commitment to the human race of which man is an inalienable part. Absence of such positive responses would inevitably lead to the torture and isolation that American life may bring. Hence, Salinger's protagonist forms the antithesis of the "Beat Generation" who take refuge in hallucinogens in order to escape from the problems of human existence. In fact, Salinger's answer is reminiscent of the conclusion James Joyce's Stephen Dedalus reaches in A *Portrait of the Artist as a Young Man* and *Ulysses*. Dedalus thinks that he can achieve his ambition of becoming the writer he is destined to be only when he gets free of the shackles of family, Church and state. Only then will he be able to discover his true subject. On the contrary, what he discovers is that there are no subjects for fiction other than family, church and state. The lesson is reinforced in *Ulysses*, as Stephen meets Leopold Bloom, thoroughly human and thoroughly vulnerable person and learns about the power of love. Pinsker rightly observes: "I read Holden's concluding admission that he 'misses' everyone as a similar recognition." (1993:97)

Holden Caulfield symbolizes, in the early stages of the novel, *The Catcher in the Rye*, the orphaned hero who finds himself plunged again and again into the "spurious, disruptive rituals of the actual world," but resurrects himself in a willing fashion and "with marvelously inadequate equipment" takes on "as much of the world as is available to him, without ever fully submitting to any of the world's determining categories." (Lewis 1959:198) This is what makes Holden Caulfield an unforgettable exercise in self-redemption amidst the coarse and brutal ugliness of a degenerate and decadent society, putting him on a higher pedestal where all great modern American protagonists come to represent the unsullied glory of the self.

Nine Stories

N*ine Stories* is a collection of stories selected by Salinger from the later stories published between 31 January 1948. and 31 January 1953. The predicaments faced by the fictional personages in *Nine Stories* are by and large similar to those of the protagonist of *The Catcher in the Rye*. The stories portray protagonists trapped between ideals and oppressive realities. besides depicting their disgust with what is fake and phoney and their movement from despair to hope and alienation to integration with society. It is significant that the anthology opens with a story in which the protagonist commits suicide. The succeeding stories present protagonists passing through different stages: self-realization, guilt, remorse, desire for human contact and acceptance of society. The last story portrays full integration of the hero with society.

II

In "A Perfect Day for Bananafish," Seymour is already married to Muriel. His own values are intellectual and spiritual in contrast to the superficial and materialistic ones of his wife. He prefers to play the piano at the hotel where the couple is taking a holiday. while others play bingo. He enjoys reading poetry and not the popular chic magazines and. therefore. cannot help quoting T.S. Eliot during his conversation with the four-year-old Sybil. Seymour had given Muriel a book of German poems entitled *Duino Elegies* (Lane 1973:28) by Rilke who. Seymour thought. was "the *only great poet of the century*." (Salinger 1964:6)

Muriel is the very antithesis of her husband. being a shallow and snobbish girl, interested solely in appearances. The very first paragraph of the story brings out Muriel's preoccupation with appearances:

> She washed her comb and brush. She took the spot out of her beige suit. She moved the button on her Sak's blouse. She tweezed out two freshly surfaced hairs in her mole. When the operator finally rang her room, she was sitting on the window seat and had almost finished putting lacquer on the nails of her left hand. (3)

Her snobbishness and shallowness are revealed in her contemptuous attitude towards those who do not look smart and chic. Talking to her mother over the phone, she says: "We couldn't get the room we had before the war. . . . The people are aweful this year. You should see what sits next to us in the dining room. At the next table. They look as if they drove down in a truck." (9) Muriel acquires her knowledge about life by reading cheap magazines and is seen reading "an article in a women's pocket-size magazine called 'Sex is Fun or Hell.'" (3) She talks mockingly of the book of German poems during her telephonic conversation with her mother, who fully matches her in sheer vulgarity and artificiality. Consequently, Seymour calls his wife "Miss Spiritual Tramp of 1948." (5) During this long-distance telephonic conversation with Muriel, her mother's shallowness and stupidity get repeatedly asserted through trivial enquiries like, "How's your blue coat?" and "How are the clothes this year?" (8) Nor are the other people in the story any better. Mrs. Carpenter and her interlocutor Mrs. Hubbel, staying at the same hotel, talk about the "silk handkerchief" some woman was wearing and Mrs. Hubbel says, "I wish I knew how she tied it. It was actually darling." (11) The adult world fills Seymour with total revulsion and he turns to children. At the beach, he spends time conversing with a four-year-old child, Sybil. Seymour's opinion of Muriel is expressed in his reply to Sybil's question, "Where is the lady?" He answers, "That's hard to say, Sybil. She may be in any one of a thousand places. At the hair-dresser's. Having her hair dyed mink. Or making dolls for poor children, in her room." (12) Thinking that children are uncorrupted, he strikes a rapport with Sybil and successfully communicates with her at her own level. Sybil asks Seymour:

> "Did you read 'Little Black Sambo'?" she said.
>
> "It's very funny you ask me that," he said. "It so happens I just finished reading it last night." He reached down and took back Sybil's hand. "What did you think of it?" he asked her.
>
> "Did the tigers run all around that tree?"
>
> "I thought they'd never stop. I never saw so many tigers."
>
> "There were only six," Sybil said.
>
> "*Only* six!" said the young man. "Do you call that *only*?"
>
> "Do you like wax?" Sybil asked.
>
> "Do I like what?" asked the young man.
>
> "Wax."
>
> "Very much, Don't you?" Sybil nodded.
>
> "Do you like olives?" she asked.
>
> "Olives—yes. Olives and wax. I never go anyplace without them." (14-15)

However, he finds that even children are not free from the taints of jealousy, possessiveness and cruelty. Sybil complains to Seymour about his having let Sharon Lipschutz, another child at the hotel, sit on the "piano seat" with him, and asks him to "push her off" next time. Seymour realizes that the Sharons of the world, though not "mean or unkind" soon turn into Sybils, who poke little dogs with balloon sticks. And Sybils, who are at least spontaneous and honest finally grow into Muriels. (Lane 1973:30) The protagonist loves Sybil for being a bright child but discovers her inadequacies and sees in her "the seedling of a future Muriel." (31)

Therefore, Seymour regards the whole civilization as spiritually barren, and morally bankrupt. This is why Eberhard Alsen observes that Seymour's allusion to *The Waste Land* is indicative of his despair as he "does not even see any hope in children." (1983:13) No wonder, the highly sensitive hero finds himself an alien in a world where ladies wear "zink salve" on their noses. Despair overwhelms him in a world in which Muriel's "room smelled of new calf-skin luggage and nail-lacquer remover." (18) Seymour has nothing in common with such a world.

Read in this self-contained way, the story conveys a pessimistic message. Salinger shows awareness of the oppressive and destructive forces in the contemporary society which drive a sensitive person like Seymour to despair and suicide.

However, a close reading of "A Perfect Day for Bananafish" reveals that the protagonist makes several attempts to integrate himself with society. He tries to drive the car carefully, besides attempting to establish contact with society through children. But he remains unsuccessful. The parable of the Bananafish in the story becomes instrumental in shedding light on the cause of Seymour's death. Bananafish are extremely fond of bananas and, therefore, swim into a hole containing lots of bananas. Having over-eaten bananas, they become so fat that they cannot swim out of the hole and, consequently, die. Like the Bananafish, Seymour, having excessively fed himself on spiritual experiences, finds himself unable to swim out of the spiritual hole into the mundane world of everyday life and dies. This interpretation of Seymour's suicide gains further credence in the light of Salinger's later fiction *Franny and Zooey, Raise High the Roof Beam, Carpenters; and Seymour: An Introduction* and "Hapworth 16, 1924," in which the novelist portrays Seymour as incapable of hatred and revulsion. Tracing the events in Seymour's life in the later works, Salinger struggles hard to establish that Seymour's suicide was caused neither by revulsion against society nor did it constitute an act of escape. Buddy Glass, the fictional narrator in *Raise High the Room Beam Carpenters; and Seymour: An Introduction*, confesses his inability to have portrayed the essential Seymour, bringing out the inherent traits of the hero's character and personality in "A Perfect Day for Bananafish." Consequently, there are differences in characterization of the Seymour of the earlier story and the Seymour of the later works. Eberhard Alsen rightly holds that because "Salinger makes Buddy take the responsibility for the differences in the characterization of Seymour in 'Bananafish' and in the later stories, he [Salinger] suggests that we ought to treat 'Bananafish' as a story told by an unreliable narrator." (1983:9) Buddy's own reactions to Muriel and the type of society Seymour finds himself in, get attributed to Seymour in the story, thus falsifying the actual Seymour.

"Uncle Wiggily in Connecticut" is a study in degeneration of the self and crumbling relationships. Eloise, the protagonist has "succumbed to the material comforts of the phoney world" (French 1963:23) by marrying Lew and, consequently, becomes bitter, cruel and guilt-ridden. Having lost the "nice" world of love with Walt Glass, she feels isolated and frustrated with her husband Lew, who deceived her as he claimed having read Jane Austen, but actually used to enjoy only cheap popular stuff. Her bitterness and frustration come out in her refusal to accede to her husband's wish to meet him with the car on account of the foul weather. This bitterness in her attitude gets further illustrated in her insensitive response to the news of her former teacher, Dr. Whiting's death from cancer, and in the cruel treatment of her daughter, Ramona. Eloise's cruel treatment of Ramona is revealed in her not allowing Ramona to sleep on one side of the bed with her new imaginary boy-friend, Mickey Mickeranno. Eloise asks Ramona:

> "Why are you sleeping way over here?"
> "Because," said Ramona.
> "Because why? Ramona I don't feel like—"
> "Because I don't want to hurt Mickey."
> "*Who*?"
> "Mickey," said Ramona, rubbing her nose. "Mickey Mickeranno."
> Eloise raised her voice to a shriek. "You get in the center of that bed. *Go on*."
> Ramona extremely frightened, just looked up at Eloise.
> "All right." Eloise grabbed Ramona's ankles and half lifted and half pulled her over to the middle of the bed. Ramona neither struggled nor cried; she let herself be moved without actually submitting to it. (37)

Ramona's loneliness and desolation become clear from her description of Jimmy Jimmereeno who has "No mommy and no daddy," (26) because the words equally apply to her own state, metaphorically. She is a totally neglected and ignored child.

The atmosphere of the story reflects the moral and spiritual degradation of the protagonists, Eloise and her friend, Mary Jane, which presents a stark contrast to Seymour's surfeit of spirituality. For example, the weather in the story is foul and outside the room in Eloise's house "the filthy slush was visibly turning to ice." (22) The lunch being cooked gets burnt and Mary Jane's employer, Mr. Weyinburg suffers from hernia. The education of Eloise and Mary Jane has been a failure and their love affairs have also flopped. Both the women do not succeed in graduating, nor are they able to attain happiness in their love affairs. As the novelist derisively observes that besides being former college roommates,

> They had an even stronger bond between them: neither of them had graduated. Eloise had left college in the middle of her sophomore year, in 1942, a week after she had been caught with a soldier in a closed elevator on the third floor of her residence hall. Mary Jane had left—same year, same class, almost the same month—to marry an aviation cadet stationed in Jacksonville, Florida, a lean, air-minded boy from Dill, Mississippi, who had spent two of the three months Mary Jane had been married to him in jail for stabbing an M.P. (20)

Their conversation revolves around trivial and superficial topics, such as, the colour of a common friend, Lieringer's hair, with no real communication between the two. It is reminiscent of the jejune conversations between Muriel and her mother (over the phone) and Mrs. Carpenter and Mrs. Hubbel in "A Perfect Day for Bananafish." Obviously, the world to which Eloise and Mary Jane belong is a world that "desire totally rejects: the world of . . . bondage and pain and confusion; . . . the world also of perverted or wasted work," (Fry 1957:147) thereby indicating that the humans who operate in such an atmosphere remain initially oblivious of their dehumanization.

However, Eloise becomes conscious of her bitchiness towards her lonely, helpless and suffering daughter soon after she heartlessly scolds Ramona over her imaginary "beau," Mickey Mickeranno. This self-realization is followed by her affectionate gesture of picking up Ramona's glasses, pressing them against her cheeks and weeping over her cruelty. "She stopped over" Ramona's bed and "losing her balance, . . . began to tuck in the blankets of Ramona's bed. Ramona was awake. She was crying and had been crying. Eloise kissed her wetly on the mouth and wiped the hair out of her eyes and then left the room." (37) Her potential ability to come out of her moral degeneration gets further revealed in her remorseful query to her friend, Mary Jane, which actually is her soliloquy: "I was a nice girl, wasn't I?" (38)

"Just Before the War with the Eskimos" also focuses on human relationships under strain and about to fall apart. Ginnie Mannox and Selena, the two friends, have been playing tennis for some time. Ginnie has been mostly paying the fare for the taxi they take for getting back home. Having been riled at this, she quarrels with Selena and insists on the latter's sharing the fare, putting tremendous strain on their friendly relationship. But through Selena's uncouth, unkempt and clumsy brother, Franklin, who affectionately insists on Ginnie taking a half chicken sandwich, thinking she must be hungry, their relationship is saved.

On the fifth Saturday, as the cab turns towards Selena's house, Ginnie speaks up: "I don't feel like getting stuck for the whole cab fare again today. . . . I'm not a millionaire, ya know." (40) Selena responds unpleasantly, "I always bring the tennis balls, don't I?" (40) This makes Ginnie angry and she retorts, "Your father *makes* them or something. . . . They don't cost *you* anything. I have to pay for every single little—" (40) Selena cuts her short, "All right, all right. . . . I only have thirty-five cents. . . . Is that enough?" (40) Ginnie says, "No, I'm sorry, but you owe me a dollar sixty-five. I've been keeping track of every—" (41) Interrupting Ginnie, Selena says, "I'll have to go upstairs and get it from my mother. Can't it wait till *Monday*? I could bring it to *gym* with me if it'd make you happy." (41) Ginnie refuses the proposal and their relationship comes to the verge of collapse:

> In hostile silence, the girls stared out of the opposite windows until the cab pulled up in front of Selena's apartment house. Then Selena, who was seated nearest the curb, let herself out. Just barely leaving the cab door open, she walked briskly and obliviously, like visiting Hollywood royalty, into the building. Ginnie, her face burning, paid the fare. She then collected

> her tennis things—racket, hand towel, and sun hat—and followed Selena. (41)

Ginnie, striding up to the elevator says, "That makes a dollar ninety you owe me." (41) The following exchange of hot words appears to have sundered their friendship:

> "I never in my life would've thought you could be so small about anything," said Selena, who was just angry enough to use the word 'small' but not quite brave enough to emphasize it.
>
> "Now you know," said Ginnie, and opened a copy of *Vogue* in front of her face. (42)

However, the arrival of Franklin on the scene acts as a redemptive force. On coming to know that Ginnie has come to their house straight from the tennis court, he solicitously asks her: "How 'bout a glass of milk?" (46) and forcing her to take the half chicken-sandwich, he says: "*Take* it for Chrissake I didn't poison it or anything." (50) Franklin's bedraggled appearance, his affectionate sensitivity and concern for others, and his bleeding finger, raise him to the pedestal of Christ. His suffering from a heart ailment becomes symbolic of his love in a largely loveless society. His simple heart cannot understand the rationale behind wars. Commenting on the stupidity of the human mind, he derisively observes, "We're gonna fight the Eskimos next. Know that?" (48)

Franklin's Christian values have a transformative effect on Ginnie's heart. Selena's having changed from her shorts into a dress—"a fact that ordinarily would have annoyed Ginnie" (54)—does not irritate her. The following conversation fully reveals the complete change of heart in Ginnie and their relationship becoming stronger and more affectionate:

> "I don't want the money anyway," Ginnie said, keeping her voice down so that she was heard only by Selena.
>
> "What?"
>
> "I've been thinking. I mean you bring the tennis balls and all, all the time. I forgot about that."

"But you said that because I didn't have to pay for them—"

"Walk me to the door," Ginnie said, leading the way. . . .

"But I thought you said you were going to the movies tonight and you needed the money and all!" Selena said in the foyer.

"I'm too tired," Ginnie said. She bent over and picked up her tennis paraphernalia.

"Listen. I'll give you a ring after dinner. Are you doing anything special tonight? Maybe I can come over." (54)

Ginnie's saying to Selena that "I met your brother," makes it abundantly clear that the change in her has been wrought through him. Franklin being represented as Christ in the story, the half chicken-sandwich acquires the sanctity of Eucharist and, therefore, Ginnie decides not to throw it away.

"The Laughing Man" contains a story within a story and the contrast in the attitude of the two protagonists, John Gedsudski and the Laughing Man, is crucial to Salinger's concept of man. John Gedsudski, the chief of the Commanche Club, takes children out for playing games and narrates the fable of the Laughing Man. Gedsudski loves Mary Hudson and the Laughing Man loves his wolf, Black Wing, dwarf Omba, a giant Mongolian, Hong and a gorgeous Eurasian girl—"The blindly loyal confederates." (61) Mary Hudson, an "unclassifiably great beauty at first sight," (63) has been meeting Gedsudski regularly for some time when he takes children out for games. Once when the children are playing, she is seen "sitting on a bench . . . sandwiched between two nursemaids with baby carriages." (69) Unlike other times she does not play, and looks sulky. She and Gedsudski have a talk, but she becomes angry. "The Chief had hold of the beaver coat" she is wearing, "but she got away from him." (70)

The imagery of "nurse-maids" and "baby-carriages" suggests Mary Hudson's pregnancy. Gedsudski's love for her demands acceptance of responsibility on his part for which he is not prepared. Mary Hudson is seen running away in tears, from the playground, by the narrator whereas "The Chief didn't go after her. He just stood watching her disappear." (71) In sharp contrast to Gedsudski's refusal to accept responsibility for his love, the protagonist of the story he tells the children, the Laughing Man, sacrifices his life for his dear Wolf, Black Wing, because of his "high sense of loyalty" towards those he loved. Dufarge, the famous French detective could never succeed in killing the Laughing Man, if the latter had not felt heart-broken at the death of Black Wing, whom the Dufarges had deceitfully killed. Salinger censures Gedsudski's callousness towards his beloved and extolls the Laughing Man's selfless sacrifice through a glaring contrast. Gedsudski's nauseating selfishness in refusing to marry Mary Hudson even after making her pregnant presents the very antithesis of the Laughing Man's altruistic nature and the manner in which he later dies.

"Down at the Dinghy" focuses on the development of the consciousness of Boo Boo Tannenbaum's four-year-old son Lionel who, having felt piqued at his Jewish father being referred to as "kike" by their maid-servant, Sandra, runs away from home and is found sitting on a dinghy. Rupp's opinion that "protection from reality is the point of the story" (1970:121) is totally wrong because the crux of the story lies in Boo Boo's efforts at preparing the child to face the squalor in the world. Referring to Sandra's remark, Boo Boo tells him, "Well, that isn't too terrible . . . that isn't the *worst* thing that could happen." (86) Furthermore, Lionel's act of throwing into water his uncle Seymour's glasses is symbolic of his desire to look at the world with his own and not anybody else's eyes. Through the portraiture of young Lionel, Salinger emphasizes the value of self awareness in acquiring capacity to face a hostile world.

"For Esme—With Love and Squalor" sketches the journey Sgt. X performs from despair, nervous breakdown and isolation to hope, health and acceptance of responsibility. It traces the root of the malaise that turns life into hell and specifically focuses on "love" which acts as a redeeming and therapeutic force to take the alienated and suffering protagonist out of his existential hell. The story, with its "triumphantly affirmative conclusion" (French 22) establishes "the transformative powers of love." (Wenke 1981:252)

There are many forces that push Sgt. X into the hell of his isolation, eventually bringing about his nervous breakdown. His wife is a superficial woman whose banality is reminiscent of Muriel's in "A Perfect Day for Bananafish." His mother-in-law,

Mrs. Grencher, matches her daughter's inanity besides being overbearing. The hero's brother's concern for Sgt. X is confined only to getting the latter to send a couple of "bayonets" and "Swastikas" as souvenirs for his children. Throughout the war, the protagonist has had to suffer the company of loutish, insensitive and idiotic Clay, Sgt. X's jeep partner in the war, who is so shameless as to make Sgt. X improve upon love-letters to his fiancee, Loretta.

Like Ettore in Hemingway's *A Farewell to Arms* (1967:126), war for Clay provides an opportunity to win medals. Once during his association with Hemingway, Salinger watched Hemingway shoot a chicken without any reason. Similarly, Clay casually shoots the cat who had once jumped on to the bonnet of the jeep Clay and Sgt. X were travelling in. The book that Sgt. X discovers in his room is *Die Zeet Ohne Beispiel*, written by a misanthrope, Joseph Goebbels, who wrote in his diary: "I have learned to despise the human being from the bottom of my soul. He makes me sick in the stomach." (Blotner 1958:5) The inscription in the book by the unmarried daughter of the owner of the house (where Sgt. X and Clay are putting up) who had worked for the Nazi party, runs: "Dear God, life is hell." (105) The protagonist's moral revulsion against an inane, selfish, loveless and brutal world throws him into intense isolation from which he can come out only if he comes across evidence showing that selfless love has not become altogether extinct. He needs to know that all human relationships have not been soured by callousness, self-aggrandizement or egocentricity.

This expression of selfless love comes from Esme, a girl of about thirteen and her brother Charles. Esme, too, like Sgt. X, is lonely. She is an orphan—her mother is dead and the father, who was in the army was slain in North Africa. She and Charles live with her aunt. Sgt. X, who had seen the "ladylike" Esme, in the Church, singing in the choir, meets her again in the "civilian tearoom." She is with her younger brother, Charles, and an efficient-looking woman, "presumably her governess." Having smiled at Sgt. X, she joins him at his table. She tells him a lot about her mother and father. She is wearing an "enormous-faced" chronographic-looking wrist-watch, which Sgt. X happens to look at. She tells him that her father "gave it [wrist-watch] to me just before Charles and I were evacuated. Purely as a memento, of course."

(100) The tea-room conversation suggests that she is isolated in various ways: from Charles, her aunt, and her governess. Her isolation is suggested by the end-position in the first row at the choir and the separateness of her voice in singing. She is a sensitive, affectionate and simple-hearted girl who tells Sgt. X, "I purely came over because I thought you looked extremely lonely. You have an extremely sensitive face." (95)

Antico, however, asserts that Esme is "a precocious snob and a cold, affected, and aristocratic brat—in a word, phoney," and that "Instead of Esme's love it is Sgt. X's sense of humor that 'saves' him." (1966:327) But it is an incontrovertible fact which emerges from the story that Esme *is* capable of selfless, affectionate love. Her concern for being a loving person comes out in her question to Sgt. X: "Do you find me terribly cold?" to which the Sergeant's answer is "absolutely not—very much to the contrary in fact." (96) There is no reason to doubt Sgt. X's perception of Esme's personality. As Kirschner rightly puts it, "Esme's understanding of her father has suddenly become the understanding that the Sergeant himself is seeking. This creation in a few pages of a profound, loving sympathy, transcending not only sex but place and time in the widest sense, is Salinger's finest achievement in the story." (1973:68) Esme's act of sending her father's wristwatch, her most cherished possession, as gift to Sgt. X, becomes a supreme expression of a tender love by one who has not yet been sullied by the falsities of the adult world. The loving gift from Esme, along with her younger brother, Charles's kisses in the letter she sends, cures Sgt. X's nervous breakdown. Having got an existential insight, Sgt. X writes under the inscription by the girl in Goebbels's book the following words from Dostoyevsky's *Crime and Punishment*: "'Fathers and teachers, I ponder what is hell?' I maintain that it is the suffering of being unable to love." (105) After reading Esme's letter, he gets out of his nervous breakdown by going off to sleep. The narrator records: "You take a really sleepy man, Esme, and he always stands a chance of again becoming a man with all his fac—with all his f-a-c-u-l-t-i-e-s intact." (114) The common need of love for both Esme and Sgt. X and its fulfilment becomes Salinger's message: love is one of the most potent redemptive forces in the contemporary dystopian world.

"Pretty Mouth and Green My Eyes," is a clear and seminal illustration of Salinger's concept of man. The whole story is in the form of a long telephonic conversation between two persons, one of them being the husband of an infidel wife. In this story, the promiscuous ways of the wife, Joanie, and a setback in the highly competitive career-market, have brought about the degradation of the husband, Arthur. Arthur comes to the verge of disintegration and collapse, but his innate self-respect and sense of dignity assert themselves. He decides to face life with all the resultant consequences, with a determination to retrieve his married life, even though it is in complete shambles on account of his wife's animality. Arthur also decides to face up to the challenge of his career, in spite of having lost a case as a junior defence lawyer. Simultaneously, the story also portrays the self-realization and feeling of contempt for one's self which overtake another character, Lee. He undergoes a change at the spiritual level. At the end of the story, he has contempt for himself and for the girl in bed with him, but not for Arthur, the cuckolded husband. At the start of the phone-conversation, Lee has contempt only for Arthur.

Arthur feels upset over his wife Joanie's absence from home because he is fully aware of her promiscuity: "She always starts necking some bastard in the kitchen when she gets tanked up." (117) He rings up Lee, his superior in the firm of Lawyers, to know Joanie's whereabouts at a time when Lee is in bed with Joanie. Lee's cool and competent arguments to allay Arthur's suspicions about Joanie are countered by Arthur's observation about his degraded situation: "I practically have to keep myself from opening every goddam closet door in the apartment—I swear to God. Every night I come home, I half expect to find a bunch of bastards hiding all over the place. *El*evator boys. Delivery boys. Cops—" (119) Truth dawns on Arthur when he asks Lee if he could join him for a drink and Lee coolly but firmly dissuades him by advising him that he "should sit tight there and relax till Joanie waltzes in." (127) Instead of feeling defeated and shattered, Arthur, having called up his internal resources, firmly resolves to face the vicissitudes of life. He rings up Lee to tell him that Joanie has just returned home, praising her as being a basically nice girl. His resurrected self, having cast off its degradation and self-pity, is revealed in his confident observation:

> Anyway, I'm gonna talk to her about it tonight. Or tomorrow I mean she's helluva good kid basically, and if we *have* a chance to straighten ourselves out a little bit, we'd be goddam stupid not to at least have a go at it. While I'm at it, I'm also gonna try to straighten out this lousy bedbug mess, too. (129)

("Bedbug mess" refers to the case he has lost in court.) Simultaneous with the change in Arthur, feelings of guilt and remorse overtakc Lee. The cigarette ash that falls on Lee's chest symbolically becomes the fire and brimstone for the guilty. Lee does not allow Joanie to remove the ash from his chest thereby confessing his acceptance of the sin and a possible punishment for it.

"De Daumier-Smith's Blue Period" records the flight of a teen-aged boy from society on account of culture-shock and his eventual return to and acceptance of it, following a psychological insight. De Daumier-Smith had moved from America to Paris along with his mother and her second husband, Robert Agadganian, in 1930. Nine years later, after the death of his mother, he has to come back to New York. This proves to be a traumatic event, as Smith says, "that threw me, and threw me terribly." (131) Smith is unable to integrate himself with the American ethos and prays for being left alone. His prayer is answered and his alienation becomes more intense. His derisive perception of the contemporary America is revealed in his drawings about which he writes:

> I drew people in evening clothes stepping out of limousines on opening nights—lean, erect, super-chic couples who had obviously never in their lives inflicted suffering as a result of underarm carelessness—couples, in fact, who perhaps didn't have any underarms. I drew sun-tanned young giants in white dinner jackets, seated at white tables alongside turquoise swimming pools, toasting each other, rather excitedly, with highballs made from a cheap but ostensibly ultra-fashionable brand of rye whisky. I drew ruddy, billboard-genic children, beside themselves with delight and good health,

> holding up their empty bowls of breakfast food and pleading good-naturedly, for more. I drew laughing high-breasted girls aquaplaning without a care in the world, as a result of being amply protected against such national evils as bleeding gums, facial blemishes, unsightly hairs, and faulty or inadequate life insurance. I drew housewives who, until they reached for the right soap flakes, laid themselves wide open to straggly hair, poor posture, unruly children, disaffected husbands, rough (but slender) hands, untidy (but enormous) kitchens. (135-36)

These words expose the superficiality, inanity, and calculated malice pervading the contemporary American civilization, besides bringing out the decadence that has overtaken the Americans because of excessive commercialism.

Therefore, De Daumier-Smith escapes into Montreal by joining M. Yoshoto's Les Amis Des Vieux Maitres, a correspondence art school, in the capacity of an art instructor. But his alienation continues even here as he finds his students highly mediocre and the Yoshotos completely uncommunicative. At this his vision of the world is reflected in an entry in his diary:

> As I was returning home wherever I had spent the evening—and I do remember that it was after dark—I stopped on the side-walk outside the school and looked into the lighted display window of the orthopedic appliances shop. Then something altogether hideous happened. The thought was forced on me that no matter how coolly or sensibly or gracefully I might one day learn to live my life, I would always at best be a visitor in a garden of enamel urinals and bedpans with a sightless, wooden dummy-deity standing by in a ruptured truss. (157)

In the meantime, the talent of one of his students, sister Irma, a nun of the Order of St. Joseph, impresses him. Significantly, Sister Irma remains an abstraction because she had neither sent her photograph, nor mentioned her age in the art-school's questionnaire. Smith's attempts to chase the shadow prove abortive, since she is withdrawn from the art-school by her superior, Father Zimmerman.

The Mother Superior of Sister Irma's convent informs M. Yoshoto of Father Zimmermann's decision. At the height of Smith's despair, arising out of his complete alienation from society, a simple act of watching a girl in the show-case of the orthopaedic appliances shop brings about a crucial psychic change, totally transforming Smith's outlook. The tall, hefty girl who was changing the truss on the wooden dummy becomes conscious of being watched, blushes and in her confusion falls down. Smith's desire to help her gets thwarted by the glass-barrier as he reaches out but his fingers hit the glass. This gesture on his part is immediately followed by a vision:

> the sun came up and sped toward the bridge of my nose at the rate of ninety-three million miles a second. Blinded and very frightened—I had to put hand on the glass to keep my balance. The thing lasted for no more than a few seconds. When I got my sight back, the girl had gone from the window, *leaving behind her a shimmering field of exquisite, twice blessed, enamel flowers.* (164, italics mine)

A realization about the value of selfless universal love symbolized by nuns, dawns on Smith and he writes in his diary: "Everybody is a nun." (164) This marks the end of his chasing a mirage and entering reality. The young hero's integration with society becomes complete with his leaving Montreal, and joining Bobby, his step-father in Rhode Island, where he begins to find the "American Girls in shorts" interesting and absorbing.

Neither the foreknowledge of his death, nor his awareness of the malice, egoism and selfishness in society affects the young protagonist's involvement with life and sense of responsibility towards society in "Teddy." Born to egoistic and petty-minded and fractious parents who turn their married life into hell, the clairvoyant, young Teddy remains unruffled. Teddy, his younger sister, Booper, and his parents who are performing artists are on a voyage in a ship. His father, Mr. McArdle, tells Teddy to get off his bag, the mother says, "Stay exactly where you are, darling." (168) Not only that, she asks him to "Jump up and down," and "Crush Daddy's bag." (168) Their hostility to each other comes out in the vicious exchange of words between them:

> "You know what I'd like to do?" Mr. McArdle said. "I'd like to kick your goddam head open."
>
> "Why don't you?"
>
> "One of these days—" he began grimly. "One of these days, you're going to have a tragic, tragic heart attack," Mrs. McArdle said, with a minimum of energy. Without bringing her arms into the open she drew her top sheet more tightly around and under her body. "There'll be a small, tasteful funeral, and everybody's going to ask who that attractive woman in the red dress is, sitting there in the first row, flirting with the organist and making a holy—." (168-69)

Teddy's involvement becomes clear from his query about the timing of the word-game, played on the ship. His affectionate concern for his father's happiness comes out in his diary entry on October 27, 1952: "See if you can find daddy's army dog tags and wear them whenever possible. It won't kill you and he will like it." (179-80) The young protagonist's resolve to answer Professor Mandell's letter, in addition to getting Sven's address to meet his wife, reflect his social involvement. The last entry in the young hero's diary amply conveys Teddy's commitment to society: "Be nicer to librarian," and "Discuss some general things with him when he gets kittenish." (181)

III

"Teddy" the last story in the anthology marks the completion of the pattern of the self in relation to society: from Seymour's inability to overcome his alienation to realization of self-degeneration by Eloise, to Sgt. X's integration with society through love and eventually to Teddy's unequivocal involvement with society. Therefore, Robert Wexelblatt is wrong in his stance that "Teddy" impliedly advocates abnegations of responsibility and withdrawal from life. (1986:75) He ignores the overwhelming textual evidence obvious in the story which makes "Teddy" an unmincing testament of commitment to public responsibility.

The stories reveal Salinger's concern with evolving a viable solution to the labyrinth of a hedonistic and acquisitive society. Most of the protagonists seem to be conscious of their predicaments and register moral progress in the direction of acceptance of society and commitment to responsibility. The novelist seems to be emphatic in making out a case for the observance of healthy and humanistic values by his ideal man. The absence of such values inevitably results in degeneration and unhappiness.

Franny and Zooey

Franny and Zooey (1961) is a collection of the two stories "Franny" and "Zooey" published in *The New Yorker* in January 1955 and May 1957 respectively. Though the two stories were published with a gap of about two years, their thematic continuity makes the book a compact whole. The first part of the book deals with Franny's estrangement from society and her nervous breakdown. Her estrangement and nervous breakdown are brought about by the egoism of her boy-friend, Lane Coutell, the sham-intellectualism of the faculty of the college she goes to and the petty pursuits of people. Her mother, Bessie Glass, and father, Les Glass, become naturally worried. The second part is about her brother, Zooey's efforts, to restore her to a healthy relationship with and a desire to fulfill her moral obligations to society. In the process, Zooey also gets an insight into human existence through reflecting over his elder brother, Seymour's advice. Consequently, his own uneasy relationship with society gets transformed into a rapport with it. The point of view in the book is third person omniscient style, Salinger being the observer, and commentator. This point of view is employed to highlight the inner turmoil and conflicts being experienced by the protagonists.

In *Franny and Zooey*, Salinger's vision of the self vis-a-vis society becomes more lucid, communicative and affirmative. The protagonists of the *Nine Stories* reach different levels of self-awareness and integration with society, whereas in the present book, religion, having been rejected as a refuge, becomes a means of bringing the alienated protagonists into the fold of society and making them alive to their responsibilities. Actually, social commitment and religion become synonymous inasmuch as Salinger makes his protagonists look at the performance of their duties towards society as a religious necessity.

The crisis that Franny and Zooey have to undergo comes as a corollary to the type of education they receive as young students at the hands of Seymour and Buddy, their elder brothers. Seymour and Buddy did not want the two youngsters to be fed on classics for fear of the siblings turning into "faculty-recreation-room savants," something which happened to so many precocious children. So, they decided to tell young Zooey and Franny as much as they knew about great men—"the saints, the arhats, the bodhisattvas, the jivanmuktas—. . ." (Salinger 1964a:56-57) As Buddy says in his letter to Zooey, "That is, we wanted you both to know who and what Jesus and Gautama and Lao-tse and Shankaracharya and Huineng and Sri Ramakrishna, etc., were before you knew too much or anything about Homer or Shakespeare or even Blake or Whitman, let alone George Washington and his cherry tree or the definition of a peninsula or how to parse a sentence." (57) They conducted "home seminars" for the two children in which they discussed metaphysical topics. The two brothers thought, all this religious education would impart to Zooey and Franny pure consciousness, the "state of being where the mind knows the source of all light." (56) But what actually happens is that the great personages become Zooey's and Franny's heroes and both of them "developed very high intellectual and spiritual standards, but they also came to despise everyone who had different values." (Alsen 1983:51) Interestingly, however, the spiritual education Franny and Zooey receive makes them aware of the unjustified contempt both of them develop for other people. Consequently, both of them make conscious efforts to overcome such feelings. Zooey succeeds only partially and begins to suffer from ulcers in the stomach. Franny is completely unsuccessful, withdraws from society and has a nervous breakdown.

II

Franny's surroundings play a vital role in bringing about her estrangement from society. In college, she is taught by professors who take pains to *appear* scholarly. For example, Franny thinks that Professor Tupper "musses up" his hair in the men's room before entering the class. In the absence of a Professor, the "section men" conduct the class and being only graduate students hardly possess any scholarship. They generally spoil the author they talk about and mostly begin to lecture on the writers on whom they wrote their M.A. theses. Even the poetry written by the faculty Professors is nothing more than "syntaxy droppings." There is no mention of "wisdom" in college. The theatre department is full of exhibitionistic egoists who keep "running around feeling terribly *chari*table and *warm*. Kissing everybody and wearing their make up all over the place, and then trying to be horribly natural and friendly" (27) when their friends come backstage to see them. Her lover, Lane Coutell, is shallow, egoistic and self-centred, besides being a typical representative of promiscuity, vulgarity and superficiality in contemporary America.

Lane's egoism comes out during his wait at the platform for Franny. When the train, in which Franny is coming to meet Lane, arrives at the platform, Lane "tried to empty his face of all expression that might quite simply, perhaps even beautifully, reveal how he felt about the arriving person." (12) His manner of speaking, during their conversations at Sickler's (restaurant), is smug as he "believes he has just hit a stride where his *voice* can do absolutely no wrong." (15, italics mine) His vulgarity becomes apparent in his remark about Flaubert's writings. He remarks, "I mean, to put it crudely . . . the thing you could say he lacks is testicularity." (15) His superficiality is revealed at the restaurant, when Franny notices him sit back and briefly look "around the room with an almost palpable sense of well-being at finding himself (he must have been sure no one could dispute) in the right place with an unimpeachably right-looking girl—a girl who was not only extraordinarily pretty, but so much the better, not too categorically cashmere sweater and flannel skirt." (15)

Lane's smirking over his getting "A" grade in his paper on Flaubert begins to irritate Franny. He goes on bragging in a boring manner about not expecting such a high grade, his perceptive analysis of Flaubert's style of writing and his desire to sometime read the paper to Franny. Referring to Flaubert's style, Lane tells Franny: "I mean I didn't say anything too goddam world-shaking or anything like that. . . . I think the emphasis I put on *why* he was so neurotically attracted to the *mot juste* wasn't too bad." (16) The authorial opinion of Lane is highly revealing as according to the novelist Lane is not the sort of person who could "keep a punch line to himself for any length of time." (17) Therefore, even though he gets annoyed with Franny's irrelevant question as to whether he wants the olive, he continues in the self-satisfied strain: "This guy Brughman thinks I ought to publish the goddam paper somewhere" (17) and adds, "I mean critical essays on Flaubert and those boys are a goddam dime a dozen. . . . As a matter of fact, I don't think there have been any really incisive jobs done on him in the last." (17) He is cut short by Franny who begins to feel exasperated over his continued idiotic self-praise. Having told him that he is talking just like a "section man," Franny explains at length about these section men:

> Well, I don't know what they are around here, but where *I* come from, a section man's a person that takes over a class when the professor isn't there or is busy having a nervous breakdown or is at the dentist or something. He's usually a graduate student or something. Anyway, if it's a course in Russian Literature, say, he comes in, in his little button-down-collar shirt and striped tie, and starts knocking Turgenev for about a half hour. Then, when he's finished, when he's completely *ruined* Turgenev for you, he starts talking about Stendhal or somebody he wrote his thesis for his M.A. on. Where I go, the English Department has about ten little section men running around ruining things for people, and they're all so brilliant they can hardly open their mouths—pardon the contradiction. I mean if you get into an argument with them, all they do is get this terribly *benign* expression on their—(17-18)

Lane feels piqued and becomes angry. His supposed love for Franny having vanished, he retaliates, "You've got a goddam bug today—you know that? What the hell's the matter with you anyway?" (18) Pointing to her present mood, he says: "Your letter didn't sound so goddam destructive." (18) Franny admits that having got depressed by her surroundings, she has been in the grip of dismal thoughts. "I'm sorry. I'm aweful. . . . I've just felt so *destructive* all week. It's aweful. It's horrible." (18) However, Franny values human relationships and that is why she feels bad at her "destructive" mood. Her desire for human relationships gets revealed in her carrying with her the memento given to her by a "corny" boy. She says: "I don't know why I carry that crazy gold swizzle stick around. . . . A very corny boy gave it to me when I was a sophomore, for my birthday. He thought it was such a beautiful and inspired gift and he kept watching my face while I opened the package. I keep trying to throw it away, but I simply can't do it. I'll go to my grave with it." (30) Therefore, she is keen to get out of her "destructive" mood and dark thoughts. Her desire to get out of gloomy thoughts becomes clear by her staring at the "little blotch of . . . sunshine [on the table] with a special intensity, as if she were considering lying down in it." (18) She suggests to Lane that they close the argument about the academic excellence of the faculty in her college and to prove her affection she smiles at him. Here again, the novelist's comment is pertinent in laying bare Lane's nature: "She smiled at Lane—in a sense genuinely—and at that moment a smile in return might at least have mitigated to some small extent events that were to follow, but Lane was busy affecting a brand of detachment of his own, and chose not to smile back." (19) Franny's request to drop the argument goes unheeded and her smile at Lane remains unresponded to. Lane professes, he would be "delighted" to drop the argument, but continues to needle her because he cannot "let a controversy drop until it had been resolved in his favor." (20) Besides being conceited and vain, Lane is also a selfish individual. His realization about Franny being unwell arouses anger and prompts only selfish thoughts: "he resented and feared any signs of detachment in a girl he was seriously dating. In any case, he surely was concerned over the possibility that this bug Franny had might bitch up the whole weekend." (19) Zooey's opinion of Lane, given to his mother, Bessie, sums up Lane's character:

> Well, I hate to disillusion you, but I've sat by the hour with him and he's not sweet at all. He's a charm boy and a fake. . . . Listen, I talked with him for twenty goddam minutes

> one night while Franny was getting ready to go out, and I say he's a big nothing. . . . He was telling me he used to listen to Franny and me every week when he was a kid—and you know what he was doing, the little bastard? He was building *me* up at Franny's expense. For absolutely *no reason* except to ingratiate himself and show off his hot little Ivy League intellect. . . . Phoney. . . . Give me an honest con-man any day. (80-81)

Franny has been in the process of withdrawal from life because she cannot find a single person whom she could not just "like" but "respect." To her the concept of "success" becomes a nightmare because it results in dehumanization of men. She hates shallow smartness of those people who for ever remain eager to establish their superiority. Her tirade against the modern value-orientation is virulent and she fulminates against Lane's irritation at her not recalling Wally Campbell, who was introduced to Franny by Lane some time back. She pinpoints the inanity of the chic, modern American society:

> It's just that for four solid years I've kept seeing Wally Campbells wherever I go. I know when they're going to be *charming*, I know when they're going to start telling you some really nasty gossip about some girl that lives in your dorm, I know when they're going to ask me what I did over the summer. I know when they're going to pull up a chair and straddle it backward and start bragging in a terribly, terribly quiet voice or *name*-dropping in a terribly quiet, *casual* voice. There's an unwritten law that people in a certain social or financial bracket can name-drop as much as they like just as long as they say something terribly disparaging about the person as soon as they've dropped his name—that he's a bastard or a nymphomaniac or takes dope all the time, or *some*thing horrible. (25)

She becomes disturbed most because "Everything everybody does is so—I don't know—not *wrong* or even mean, or even stupid necessarily. But just so tiny and sad-making." (26) The reason for her feeling that way is that everybody "wants to *get* somewhere, do something distinguished and all, be somebody interesting. It's disgusting—it *is*. I don't care what anybody says." (28) Lane's smugness and his own perverse and rotten values make him regard it as a sign of fear of competition and failure in life on her part. Franny corrects him, "I'm not afraid to compete. It's just the opposite. Don't you see that? I'm afraid I *will* compete—that's what scares me." (29)

Franny understands herself and that is why she wants to take care lest she should be swept off by the current of competitiveness and ego. "That's why," she says, "I quit the Theatre Department. Just because I'm so terribly conditioned to accept everybody else's values, and just because I like applause and people to rave about me doesn't make it right. I'm ashamed of it. I'm sick of it. I'm sick of not having the courage to be an absolute nobody." (29)

Her withdrawal which had already started because of her perception of the crassness of brutal reality is precipitated on Franny's becoming conscious about the stark divergence between her spiritual values and the material and hedonistic ones of Lane. The divergence becomes more pronounced through the book, *The Way of a Pilgrim,* which Franny has been reading and carrying in her purse. The complete title of the book is *The Way of a Pilgrim and The Pilgrim Continues His Way* translated from the Russian by R.M. French. The Pilgrim's story was first discovered in manuscript form at a Greek Orthodox monastery on Mount Athos by a Russian abbot, who copied the manuscript, on the basis of which a book was published in 1884. (Panichas 1974:293) This little book concerns a Russian peasant who, after an arduous, ascetic search, finds the purifying value of Jesus Prayer: "Lord Jesus Christ, have mercy on me" and wanders about teaching it to others. Having evinced a temporary interest in the book, Lane relapses into his own egocentricity. He begins to concentrate on his food rather than pay attention to Franny's talk about the book. Salinger emphasizes the contrast between the two worlds: the world of Lane and that of the Pilgrim. Lane "was dismembering his frogs' legs," (31) while Franny is telling him about the Pilgrim who carries with him this "knapsack filled with bread and salt." (31) Lane's conceited exhibitionism about his getting an "A" in his Flaubert Paper gets juxtaposed to the Russian peasant's unassuming nature since he does not even mention his name anywhere in the book. Franny seems to admire this anonymity as Lane's bragging about the publishability of his paper is fresh in her mind. She enthusiastically informs Lane, "He never gives his name. You never know his name the whole time he's telling the story. He just tells you he's a peasant and that he's thirty-three years old and that he's got a withered arm. And that his wife is dead." (31) All this, coupled with Lane's mocking dismissal of the Jesus Prayer, brings about Franny's nervous breakdown. Her disgust gets further intensified on learning that Lane only lusts after her body. He tells her that after a while, if she gets any decent rest, he can somehow come upstairs, "I think there is a goddam back staircase. I can find out . . . you know how long it's been. . . . When was that Friday night? Why the hell early last month, wasn't it? . . . That's no good. Too goddam long between drinks. To put it crassly." (38) Consequently, Franny withdraws from the actual world into the spiritual world of Jesus Prayer, believing that it would help in changing her outlook on life and people. Franny's psychic estrangement from an external world which sustains itself on a massive system of evil also becomes clear from her desire to speak to her dead brother, Seymour. She says to Zooey, "I want to talk to Seymour." (119) This symbolizes extreme disgust with a vicious and evil world of living people.

III

The second part "Zooey" portrays the brother's attempts to make Franny come out of her depression and withdrawal. Zooey is capable of understanding Franny's predicament in view of his having been groomed by his older brothers Seymour and Buddy, like Franny was, and in view of his being an inveterate critic of the society. When Franny asks him why he wants to go to France for acting in a movie, if he likes New York very much, his answer is:

> I *go* mostly because I'm tired as hell of getting up furious in the morning and going to bed furious at night. I *go* because

I sit in judgement on every poor, ulcerous bastard I know. (100)

Zooey's comments about mediocrity of the television producers, the psychoanalysts who "adjust" people to the inanities of life, constitute serious criticism of society. But Zooey, like Franny, because of his spiritual education, feels bad at his criticism of people which seems to demoralize them. He says that there is something, "I do to people's morale downtown that I can't stand to watch much longer. I can tell you *exactly* what I do. I make everybody feel that he doesn't really want to do any good work but that he just wants to get work done that will be thought good by everyone he knows—the critics, the sponsors, the public, even his children's school-teacher. That's what I do. That's the worst I do." (110) Zooey thinks it is wrong to tear others to pieces and says to Franny (as much as to himself): "In the first place, you're way off when you start railing at *things* and people instead of at yourself. We both are. I do the same goddam thing about television—I'm aware of that. But it's *wrong*. It's *us*." (111) Being conscious of the dangers of withdrawing into his shell, on account of his trenchant criticism of others, Zooey has been making efforts to fight, though not completely successfully, the tendencies of self-absorption. A good instance of such efforts may be furnished in an incident from the text. While shaving and looking into the mirror, Zooey avoids looking directly at the reflection of his face, and instead looks directly into his own eyes, "as though his eyes were neutral territory, a no man's land in a private war against narcissism he had been fighting since he was seven or eight years old." (76) These words clearly indicate that from a fairly young age Zooey had been struggling hard to save his self from getting irretrievably bogged down in the quagmire of narcissistic absorption.

Zooey's efforts to restore Franny to a meaningful contact with society and make her take up her responsibilities with conviction are simultaneously directed at himself. For, it is essential for him to be talking with conviction to her, if she is to be restored to the world. The solution to Franny's crisis has, therefore, to be resolution of Zooey's own predicament.

Having identified the source of his own and his sister's alienation, he proceeds to explain to Franny that it is they who have to make the necessary adjustment. He tells Franny not to rant against "ego" all the time. It is not "ego" which is evil *per se.* Ego is responsible for the creation of beauty and Zooey cites the examples of Emily Dickinson and Epictetus who created poetry because of their egos. Besides, he remarks that it is difficult to determine what is "ego" and what is not, suspecting that it is not "Ego" of which Professor Tupper is guilty but some other dirtier "base faculty." Perhaps, Tupper feels insecure as a teacher and to hide his incompetence, he puts on a scholarly appearance.

Zooey is also critical of his sister's Jesus Prayer which she is using as a shield for avoiding social responsibility. He makes her realize that she is behaving the same way as the people she hates and, ironically, becoming phoney and acquisitive as anybody else. He observes:

> You talk about piling up treasure—money, property, culture. knowledge and so on and so on. In going ahead with the Jesus Prayer—just let me finish, now please—in going ahead with the Jesus Prayer, aren't you trying to lay up some kind of treasure? Something that's every goddam bit as nego*tiable as all those other, more material things? Or does the fact that it's a prayer make all the difference? I mean by that, is there all the difference in the world for you, in which side somebody lays up his treasure—thieves can't break in et cetera? (117)

For Zooey, there is no difference between the two kinds of treasure—spiritual and material treasures. Zooey further objects to his sister's use of the Jesus Prayer "to set up some little cozy, holier-than-thou trysting place with some sticky, adorable divine *personage who'll take you in his arms and relieve you of all your duties and make all your nasty *Weltschmerzen* and Professor Tuppers go away and never come back." (134) He accuses Franny of misusing the prayer to ask for a world consisting only of "dolls and saints."

Zooey enters Seymour's room with the intention of impersonating Buddy over the phone to convince Franny of the wrongness of her attitude. The attempt at impersonation fails but he succeeds in making Franny come out of her withdrawal. Salinger's emphasis on "love," "action" and "work" as redeeming forces in human existence becomes clear from the sheet nailed at the back of the door of Seymour's room on which short excerpts from the scriptures and classics are calligraphed. The excerpt from the *Bhagvad Gita*, for example, tells man that he has "the right to *work*" and exhorts him to "*Perform every action* with his eyes fixed on the Supreme Lord." (138, italics mine) There are also two quotations from Kafka. In the first one, probably taken from a Kafka story, the protagonist is asked by an acquaintance in a deserted coffee house at midnight whether the latter would like to join the former. The protagonist declines. The other quotation talks about the "happiness of being with people." (140) Both these quotations from Kafka suggest as well as confirm the living credo of the dead Seymour: man's fulfilment lies not away from humanity but in human inter-action and inter-relationships.

While unsuccessfully impersonating as Buddy over the phone, Zooey points out the contradiction in his sister's reciting the Jesus Prayer and her practical behaviour. He tells her:

> if it's the religious life you want, you ought to know right now that you're missing out an every single goddam religious action that's going on around this house. You don't even have sense enough to *drink* when somebody brings you a cup of *consecrated* (italics mine) chicken soup-which is the only kind of chicken soup Bessie ever brings to anybody around this madhouse. So just *tell* me, just tell me, buddy. Even if you went out and searched the whole world for a master—some guru, some holy man—to tell you how to say your Jesus Prayer properly, what good would it do you? How in *hell* are you going to recognize a legitimate holy man when you see one if you don't even know a cup of consecrated chicken soup when it's right in front of your nose? Can you tell me that? (152-53)

The chicken soup is consecrated with "love" of a person who has no motives in offering it to Franny. Therefore, Franny's practical behaviour comes to be irreligious.

Zooey tells Franny that she is an actress because in one of her past incarnations she wished to be a good actress. Giving her the Vedantic advice, he tells her that "The only thing you can do now, the only re*lig*ious thing you can do, is *act*." (154) She has no right to shy away from her duty. An artist's only concern is "to shoot for some kind of perfection, *and on his own terms*, not anyone else's." (155) Here Zooey is making use of Vedanta Hinduism to effect a cure of Franny's malaise. The theory of reincarnation and the concept of *karma yoga*, which are constituents of Hindu Vedantic philosophy, form parts of Zooey's advice to Franny. Birth, death and rebirth pertain to the "cycle of re-incarnation." (Vivekananda 1955:3) "The word *karma* is derived from the Sanskrit *kri*, 'to do.'" (3) The major Hindu scripture which advocates the *karma yoga* ideal is the *Bhagvad Gita*. "In the *Gita*, the Lord Krishna tells the warrior Arjuna that it is basically wrong to injure or kill any living thing; but for a warrior who fights in a righteous war, the killing of enemies is not a sin but a holy duty." (Vivekananda 1944:15) Zooey recollects an incident from his childhood when he was participating in the Radio Quiz Programme, "It's a Wise Child." Once on the eve of going for the programme, Seymour had asked him to shine his shoes for the "Fat Lady." At that time, Zooey had not understood who the Fat Lady was. But over the years, he formed a picture of the Fat Lady as a person "sitting on this porch all day, swatting flies, with her radio going full blast from morning till night . . . and she probably had cancer." (156) While talking to Franny, he gets an insight into what Seymour had meant. The "Fat Lady" becomes the symbol of the common, suffering man whom Seymour had equated with Christ. Once this revelation dawns on him, he makes Franny also aware of it by saying: "*—don't you know who that Fat Lady really is*? . . . Ah, buddy. Ah, buddy. It is Christ Himself. Christ Himself, buddy." (156) This makes Franny recall Seymour once having told her also to be funny for the "Fat Lady" and she too had not understood the nature of the advice. But now she rejoices, having realized that she has at last found the solution to her predicament. The Christ consciousness is going to be the ideal panacea for her spiritual and psychic ailments.

Richard H. Rupp suggests that the myth of the Fat Lady "absolves the Glasses from social responsibilities even as it seems to call for them. The Glasses have only to be their beautiful selves on the radio program and a charismatic relationship with the audience of Fat Ladies will follow." (1970:125) Rupp, as usual, grossly misinterprets the symbolic significance of the Fat Lady. Shining of their shoes becomes a metaphoric obligation on the Glass children not to escape their duty and to do it with a sense of dedication and commitment. The metaphor also implies being at their best while giving the performance on the radio. In agreeing to abide by Seymour's advice, the younger Glass children testify to their not getting "absolved" of social responsibilities; instead they confirm their assumption of these. The Fat Lady, as mentioned earlier, stands for the most ordinary member of the listening public and this fact makes Franny and Zooey strive consciously for a meaningful relationship with their audience, an audience of Fat Ladies.

In *Franny and Zooey*, the thematic relationship between Franny and Lane and the efforts of Zooey to effect Franny's redemption and take her out of her predicament, which sought to make her a prisoner of an existential situation, symbolize Salinger's eagerness to emphasize the resurgence of the individual when placed in a demonic human world. Zooey himself is made an instrument to effect this positive transfiguration, and while being engaged in this process a solution to his own problems dawns upon him. Effecting his sister's redemption has a catalytic impact on his own psyche and the Zooey we witness at the end of the book symbolizes an individual who epitomizes Salinger's concept of man. The crux of the concept illustrates the necessity for every right-thinking and conscious individual to develop a meaningful social interaction with other humans. To be a narcissistic self and get obsessively transfixed within one's own image in the mirror of life constitutes a dire negation of the highest principles of human existence. *Franny and Zooey* as a work becomes, thus, Salinger's potent message to every reader: be your own self and yet do remain rooted to your social environment.

Raise High the Roof Beam, Carpenters; and Seymour: An Introduction

Raise High the Roof Beam, Carpenters; and Seymour: An Introduction, first published in 1963, is a collection of the two stories originally published in *The New Yorker* on 19 November 1955 and 6 June 1959 respectively. The first part of the book, "Raise High the Roof Beam, Carpenters" is the account of Seymour Glass's marriage to Muriel. The point of view is the first person narrative. It is through Buddy Glass's consciousness that all the essential details of the situation regarding Seymour and other characters get filtered down to the reader. Buddy Glass's narrative deals retrospectively with Seymour, as the latter is already dead at the time of the narration in 1955, having committed suicide in 1948 as described in the story "A Perfect Day for Bananafish." Since no other member could attend Seymour's wedding, Boo Boo, their sister, younger to Buddy, writes to Buddy urging upon him to positively make it to the marriage coromony. Buddy, who is in the Army, manages to be present. Muriel is the daughter of Mr. and Mrs. Fedder. The large crowd of guests at the Fedders includes the bride's Matron of Honour and her husband, Mrs. Silsburn, one of Muriel's aunts, and a deaf-mute, bride's father's Uncle. This group, together with Buddy, is bunched up in a car going to the place of wedding. However, the car gets held up on account of a parade. Buddy invites them to Seymour's apartment. The Matron of Honour learns through the telephonic call she makes that Seymour and Muriel have eloped and that it is unnecessary to reach the place of wedding.

Salinger's vision of man is largely reflected in his principal protagonist Seymour Glass, who is either talked about in some of the novelist's writings or appears as a fictional persona. The concept of man Salinger seeks to convey is linked to the growth and explication of Seymour's personality. In *Franny and Zooey*, it is Seymour's ideal of universal Christian love and the Vedantic tenet of "Karma" (action) and reincarnation which eventually provide a solution to Franny's predicament and make Zooey's acceptance of society and commitment to responsibilities an outcome of his understanding. In *Raise High the Roof Beam, Carpenters; and Seymour: An Introduction*, Salinger resurrects Seymour not only to make clear the crux of "A Perfect Day for Bananafish," but also to focus on Seymour's evolution.

The Taoist tale in the beginning of the book reveals the stage of evolution in Salinger's protagonist. Buddy, the narrator, recalls Seymour having read the Taoist tale* to Franny to make her stop crying when she was only ten months old, and had been shifted to Seymour's and Buddy's room so as to keep her safe from mumps from which several others in the family were suffering. The story runs:

> Duke Mu of Chin said to Po Lo: 'You are now advanced in years. Is there any member of your family whom I could employ to look for horses in your stead?' Po Lo replied: 'A good horse can be picked out by its general build and appearance. But the superlative horse—one that raises no dust and leaves no tracks—is something evanescent and fleeting, elusive as thin air. The talents of my sons lie on a lower plane altogether; they can tell a good horse when they see one, but they cannot tell a superlative horse. I have a friend, however, one Chiu-fang Kao, a hawker of fuel and vegetables, who in things appertaining to horses is no wise my inferior. Pray see him.'
>
> Duke Mu did so, and subsequently dispatched him on the quest for a steed. Three months later, he returned with the news that he had found one. 'It is now in Shach'iu,' he added. 'What kind of a horse is it?' asked the Duke. 'Oh, it is a dun-colored mare,' was the reply. However, someone being

---

*The selection offered without citation

> sent to fetch it, the animal turned out to be a coal-black stallion! Much displeased, the Duke sent for Po Lo. 'That friend of yours,' he said, 'whom I commissioned to look for a horse, has made a fine mess of it. Why, he cannot even distinguish a beast's color or sex! What on earth can he know about horses?' Po Lo heaved a sigh of satisfaction. 'Has he really got as far as that?' he cried. 'Ah, then he is worth ten thousand of me put together. There is no comparison between us. What Kao keeps in view is the spiritual mechanism. In making sure of the essential, he forgets the homely details; intent on the inward qualities, he loses sight of the external. He sees what he wants to see, and not what he does not want to see. He looks at the things he ought to look at, and neglects those that need not be looked at. So clever a judge of horses is Kao, that he has it in him to judge something better than horses.'
>
> When the horse arrived, it turned out indeed to be a superlative animal. (Salinger 1964b:9-10)

Seymour is capable of penetrating the external surfaces and reaching the essence of people and things like Chiu-fang Kao, mentioned in the Taoist tale. Chiu-fang Kao was able to pick out a superlative horse for Duke Mu of Chin, without being even conscious of either the sex or colour of the horse. Buddy, the narrator, clearly identifies Seymour with Chiu-fang Kao when he says: "Since the bridegroom's permanent retirement from the scene, I haven't been able to think of anybody whom I'd care to send out to look for horses in his stead." (11)

II

Seymour and Buddy are placed in a dystopian world with distorted values and perverted practices. In this world sickness passes for health, sexual restraint and morality become abnormal and psychoanalysts adjust people to the joys of the *Life* magazine and Sunday television. Mrs. Fedder, who "sees a good Jungian man twice a week," (13) becomes the normal person who passes judgement on the sanity of Seymour. As Seymour records in his diary,

Muriel's mother, Mrs. Fedder, thinks that "apparently there is something 'wrong' with me because I haven't seduced Muriel." (56) In such a milieu, chic mediocrity gets extolled, becoming an admirable trait. The Matron of Honor offers paeans of praise to Mrs. Fedder when she says: "I honestly think she's one of the few really brilliant people I've met in my entire life. I mean she's read just about everything that's ever been printed. My gosh, if I'd read just about one-tenth of what that woman's read and for*go*tten, I'd be happy." (31-32) For Seymour and Buddy, it is a world, part of which is hostile, part indifferent and the rest deaf. The hostility of this world is hurled at Seymour (also at Buddy) through the Matron of Honour, the spokeswoman of all those people who hate precocious children. Seymour and Buddy as also the other children of the family, including the youngest, Zooey and Franny, having been precocious children, participated in a radio quiz programme called, 'It's a Wise Child.' The Matron of Honour fumes at Buddy in the car: "If you're interested . . . that was the one programme on the air I always absolutely loathed. I loathe precocious children. If I ever had a child that—." (37-38) Her hatred becomes rabid as she works herself up into a towering rage against Seymour who, she thinks, (on the authority of Mrs Fedder) is a sadist and a latent homosexual. She angrily declares: "I'd like to get my hands on him [Seymour] for about *two minutes*. Just *two minutes*, that's all." (20) These words clearly imply that the Matron of Honour epitomizes sheer unadulterated malice exhibited by shallow chic society against people like Seymour, who possess intellectual capabilities. Her attack on Seymour continues when she rhetorically asks Mrs. Silsburn: "Does that sound like a normal—a normal *man*—to you? Or does it sound like somebody that's either *never grown* up or is just an absolute raving maniac of some crazy kind?" (35)

The Matron of Honor is prompted to ask this question on account of Seymour's telling his fiancee to postpone their marriage till he feels less happy. The Matron of Honor advertizes to the world Seymour's cruelty in having hit Charlotte Mayhew, when she was young "and she had nine stitches taken in her face." (35) In 1955, she had become a famous actress. The Matron of Honor traces the genesis of Seymour's alienation in his having been a participant in the radio programme, 'It's a Wise Child,' because the publicity such children get distorts their personality and renders them incapable of maintaining meaningful relationships. Mrs. Silsburn and Matron of Honor's husband, the Lieutenant, form the indifferent part of the world, evincing little interest in what Buddy tells them about his brother, Seymour.

The third part of the world Buddy finds himself in is constituted by the little old man, who is deaf and mute. Eventually, when everyone else has left Seymour's apartment, only the deaf-mute remains there. Significantly, Buddy finds his audience only in this deaf-mute to whom he explains why Seymour, who was only twelve then, had thrown a stone at Charlotte. "Would you like to know how Charlotte got those nine stitches?" Buddy asks the deaf-mute Uncle, and answers, "We were up at the Lake. Seymour had written to Charlotte, inviting her to come up and visit us, and her mother finally let her. What happened was, she sat down in the middle of our driveway one morning to pet Boo Boo's cat, and Seymour threw a stone at her. He was twelve. That's all there was to it. He threw it at her because she looked so beautiful sitting there in the middle of the driveway with Boo Boo's cat." (69) He was highly excited about the extremely beautiful sight and the act was the consequence of sheer excitement of a young boy. Irving Malin is also of the view that Seymour as a "child throws a stone at a girl because he wants to express his love." (Malin 1962:32)

Even Buddy is confused about Seymour's motives in marrying Muriel because Boo Boo in her letter to Buddy says about Muriel: "She's a zero in my opinion but terrific-looking." (13) Seymour's diary which Buddy finds in the bathroom helps clear Buddy's confusion about his brother's motives in marrying such a shallow person. The picture that emerges in his diary makes Seymour out to be a poet, saint and seer, who is compassionate, sensitive, aware of and alive to beauty and holds forth the cardinal value of love and assumption of responsibilities. Seymour is quite aware of the mediocrity of Mrs. Rhea Fedder who cannot rise above banalities. He writes in his diary, "Sometimes when I leave, I have a peculiar feeling that both M. and her mother have stuffed my pockets with little bottles and tubes containing lipstick, rouge, hair nets, deodorants, and so on. I feel overwhelmingly grateful to them but I don't know what to do with their invisible gifts." (55) Mrs. Fedder is irritating and opinionated, "deprived, for life, of any understanding or taste for the main current of poetry that flows through all things, all things. She might as well be dead, and yet she goes on living, stopping at delicatessens, seeing her analyst, consuming a novel every night, putting on her girdle, plotting for Muriel's health and prosperity." (57) But in spite of all this Seymour does not dislike her. On the contrary, he writes: "I love her. I find her unimaginatively brave." (57) These words of Seymour again confirm the Taoist theory of essences as exemplified in the story of Chiu-fang Kao. Seymour is able to disregard the irritating external traits of Mrs. Fedder's character and perceives her bravery in spite of her shallowness.

Being cognizant of his own flaws, he rues them. It saddens Seymour to hurl his learning at Muriel because it hurts her. Seymour and Muriel go to see *Mrs. Miniver*, a war movie with Greer Garson, and Seymour writes:

> She looked over at me when the children in the picture brought in the kitten to show to their mother. M. loved the kitten and wanted me to love it. Even in the dark, I could sense that she felt the usual estrangement from me when I don't automatically love what she loves. Later, when we were having a drink at the station, she asked me if I didn't think that kitten was "rather nice." When did I ever frighten her out of her normal vocabulary? Bore that I am, I mentioned R.H. Blyth's definition of sentimentality: that we are being sentimental when we give to a thing more tenderness than God gives to it. I said (sententiously?) that God undoubtedly loves kittens, but not, in all probability, with Technicolor bootees on their paws. He leaves that creative touch to script writers. (53-54)

Muriel does not like the remark and feels "unclose" to Seymour for a while. Seymour becomes full of self-reproach at having used his knowledge to destroy the simple-hearted joy Muriel derives out of life. He reflects: "The human voice conspires to desecrate everything on earth." (54) Muriel's habit of not dissecting her feelings and thoughts and, on the contrary, following her instincts and impulses, makes her truly *human*, and Seymour prizes her for that: "He is attracted to her because, unlike Buddy, he is able to see her simplicity and naturalness as very positive qualities which he himself lacks and greatly needs." (Alsen 1980:44)

Being fully aware of his "perfection complex," his inability to "go beyond poetry" and lead a life of "indiscrimination," Seymour, in Eberhard Alsen's words, laments that "sophistication and erudition have estranged him from ordinary humanity and have made him unable to relate to 'normal people.'" (46)

Muriel seems to him to be just the appropriate life-partner who tries to teach him "to smile, spreading the muscles around my mouth with her fingers," making Seymour exclaim with joy, "How beautiful it is to see her laugh. Oh, God, I'm so happy with her." (56) Seymour feels happy that Muriel "has an undying, basically undeviating love for the institution of marriage itself. She has a primal urge to play house permanently." (56-57) He writes about her motives for marriage: "She wants to get a very dark sun tan and go up to the desk in some very posh hotel and ask if her husband has picked up the mail yet. She wants to shop for curtains. She wants to shop for maternity clothes. She wants to get out of her mother's house, whether she knows it or not, and despite her attachment to her. She wants children—good-looking children, with her features, not mine. I have a feeling, too, that she wants her own Christmas-tree ornaments to unbox annually, not her mother's." (57)

As if Seymour could foresee that Buddy would read his diary, he writes about Buddy's reaction to Muriel: "I think of him as I write about Muriel. He would despise her marriage motives as I've put them down here. But are they despicable? In a way they must be, but yet they seem to me so human-size and beautiful that I can't think of them even now as I write this without feeling deeply, deeply moved." (57)

By marrying Muriel, an ordinary girl, Seymour hopes to join the mainstream of life, simultaneously pointing to his younger brothers and sisters who regard him as their "guru" the dangers of excessive erudition and intellectualism.

After Mrs. Helen Silsburn alludes to the physical likeness of

Charlotte and Muriel, Buddy further understands Seymour's motive in marrying Muriel. "Seymour may be drawn to Muriel, for example, by his conscious or unconscious desire to atone for the injury he caused her look-alike, Charlotte." (Alsen 1980:45) Finally, Seymour's entry in the diary stating that his marrying Muriel gives him "The joy of *responsibility* for the first time in my life," (70, italics mine) is significant from the point of view of the crucial change in him vis-a-vis society. Seymour himself refers to the change in his statement: "I feel as though I'm about to be born." (70) He has taken a step which will change the whole course of his life. He agrees with and admires the Vedantic view of marriage: "Marriage partners are to serve each other. Elevate, help, teach, strengthen each other, but above all, *serve*." (70) Buddy's consciousness also registers a change. He now understands Seymour's motives in marrying Muriel. He also understands why Seymour had asked Muriel to postpone the wedding and why he was absent at the time of the wedding. Seymour was indeed so excessively happy at the prospect of the tremendous change that his marriage to Muriel would bring in his life that he wrote, "I'm too keyed up to be with people." (70) This "inner change, his acceptance of Seymour's reasons for marrying Muriel is the key to the meaning of 'Carpenters.'" (Alsen 1980:46) Buddy's decision to send the deaf-mute's cigar with a "*blank sheet* enclosed, by way of explanation" (71, italics mine) is symbolic of his having given a clean chit to Seymour for eloping with Muriel and marrying her. Dennis L. O'Connor also holds somewhat similar opinion about the blank paper as he believes that the blank sheet of paper suggests Buddy's forgiveness of Seymour. Transcending judgemental language, Buddy's wordless gesture is indicative of a movement toward renunciation of his anger and the related desire to control Seymour. (1984: 316-32)

The world Seymour exists in may be hostile, indifferent or deaf but he has reached a stage where he not only co-exists with society but lives a "good life." McSweeny says that Seymour becomes "almost palpable representative of higher life" and "Even his metaphorical stigmata—'I have scars on my hands from touching certain people' . . . seems to me a striking evocation of what George Eliot called 'a keen vision and feeling of all ordinary life.'" (McSweeny 1978:65)

III

In the second part "Seymour: An Introduction," Salinger continues the exposition of Seymour's character through the fictional narrator, Buddy Glass. This part of the book is prefaced by two quotations:

> The actors by their presence always convince me, to my horror, that most of what I've written about them until now is false. It is false because I write about them with steadfast love (even now, while I write it down, this, too, becomes false) but varying ability, and this varying ability does not hit off the real actors loudly and correctly but loses itself fully in this love that will never be satisfied with the ability and therefore thinks it is protecting the actors by preventing this ability from exercising itself.
>
> It is, (to describe it figuratively) as if this clerical error became conscious of being such. Perhaps, this was no error but in a far higher sense was an essential part of the whole exposition. It is, then, as if this clerical error were to revolt against the author, out of hatred for him, were to forbid him to correct it, and were to say, 'No, I will not be erased, I will stand as a witness against thee, that thou art a very poor writer.' (75)

The first quotation is from Kafka and the other from Kierkegaard. Both the quotations highlight a writer's predicament vis-a-vis his writing material. Buddy mentions these in order to convey the arduousness of his own task as a writer.

"Seymour: An Introduction" is as much Buddy's story as it is Seymour's. Even as Buddy grapples with his task of unravelling the real Seymour, he has to pass through despair. As his narrative progresses, his own understanding of Seymour increases. Finally, Buddy reaches his moment of epiphany, discerns the sacredness of human relationships and the piousness involved in the assumption of social responsibilities. The narrative goes back further in time than even the first part of the book and presents Seymour as a young boy, youth and adult. While on the one hand, Seymour's saintliness is confirmed, Buddy himself finds a solution to his own predicament. The point of view continues to be first person narrative. The stance of the narrator is ironic. The structure is formless, in keeping with the unconventional nature of the subject—Seymour. Seymour's personality is explored in all its aspects—as artist (poet), brother, son, saint, critic, seer, and human being.

Salinger takes pains to identify himself with the narrator, Buddy Glass, as the latter lays claim to having written *The Catcher in the Rye*, "Teddy" and "A Perfect Day for Bananafish." The style of the book is informal whereby Buddy establishes a close relation with the reader by addressing him directly and putting in certain asides. Buddy involves the reader with the process of writing with a view to winning credibility for the protagonist—Seymour—whose life and personality are intractable and elusive. In the "entre-nous" spirit that he creates between his reader and himself, he presents Seymour as he has known him.

Seymour's saintliness becomes transparently clear in the second part of the book. In fact, all the aspects of his personality reflect his saintliness. The contemporary destructive forces have their go at Seymour. Buddy reports that when Seymour was eleven years old, he was "examined by a reputable group of professional Freudians for six hours and forty-five minutes." (79) Referring to Seymour's inherent goodness, Buddy says that Seymour was an "undefeatable champion talker" among all the Glass members but "he passionately yearned to see one or another of us outpoint or simply outlast him in a conversation." (86) The image of "curlew sandpiper" used for Seymour by Buddy indicates Seymour's elusiveness. The Chinese and Japanese poetry are known not only to be musical, and enlightening but also for their contact with life. A Chinese or Japanese poet does not live in the ivory tower of art; his "real forte is knowing a good persimmon or a good crab or a good mosquito bite on a good arm," (91) and his poetry reflects his intense contact with life. Seymour's interest in Chinese and Japanese poetry proves his own predilection for life and not art, even though he is an artist. He is an extremely bad performer at team games, not from lack of ability but from misplacement of it and not from lack of team work but surfeit of it, being unable to "understand the overriding importance of competition" and wanting "to extend the cooperative spirit of teamwork to opponents as well as team mates." (Boe 1987:69)

It becomes improbable for such a person to withdraw from life because he finds it disgusting and unbearable. The story "A Perfect Day for Bananafish" portrays Seymour as an irritable, churlish and withdrawn individual because of the squalid reality. But Buddy confesses his failures in properly describing Seymour on paper over the past eleven years. He admits to having written and burned "at least a dozen stories or sketches about him since 1948" (135) on account of his dissatisfaction with the authenticity of Seymour's portrayal. Buddy is dissatisfied with "A Perfect Day for Bananafish," too. Testifying to the falseness of Seymour who "did the walking and talking in that early story, not to mention the shooting," Buddy says that he "was not Seymour at all." (87) Falseness in the portrayal of Seymour is facetiously ascribed by Buddy to the fact that he "was using a very poorly rehabilitated, not to say unbalanced, German typewriter at the time." (87) Even members of his own family pointed out to Buddy that the Seymour of the story "A Perfect Day for Bananafish" resembled himself more rather than the real Seymour.

Tracing the cause of Seymour's suicide, Buddy says: "I say that the true artist-seer, the heavenly fool who can and does produce beauty, is mainly dazzled to death by his own scruples, the blinding shapes and colors of his own scared human conscience." (82) Seymour, as an artist, is morally scrupulous and unable to compromise with the corruption of society. However, as a man, he is sensitive and compassionate. Both these aspects, coming into contact with a phoney and disgusting society, create an excruciating feeling which lacerates and hurts Seymour's psyche. Therefore, it is wrong to hold that Seymour committed suicide because of his hatred and disgust for Mrs. Fedder, or Muriel or Sybil.

Seymour was, in any case, incapable of hatred. He was a saint and a seer who had imbibed religious tenets of Christianity, Zen Buddhism, Classical Taoism and Advaita Vedanta. His universal love comes from Christianity. He tells Buddy that Christ had said "Call no man Fool," because there are no fools in society. Likewise, his egolessness and detachment come from Zen Buddhism. Buddy recalls Seymour's complete unconcern for victory or defeat while playing a game. Seymour never bothered to play any game in its proper manner, because he played the game for the joy of playing it. In Buddy's words: "I was generally dazed into colorlessness when I played ping-pong with Seymour. It was like having Mother Kali herself on the other side of the net, multi-armed and grinning, and without a particle of interest in the score." (144) When Seymour, as a young boy, played marbles and his marble shot someone else, "he would be all smiles when he heard a responsive click of glass striking glass, but it never appeared to be clear to him *whose* winning click it was. And it's also a fact that someone almost invariably had to pick up the marble he'd won and *hand* it to him." (154) This becomes analogous to Holden's attitude towards games. He dislikes the football game being played at his school ground on account of its becoming a source of bitterness through victory and defeat, rather than promoting the fellow feeling of sharing the joy of the game. Seymour's remarkable capacity to "free himself of the surface of things and to penetrate into matter in order to lay bare its ultimate structures" (Eliade 1965:23) is a product of Taoist influence. His belief in incarnations and his considering action ("Karma") as sacred illustrate the influence of Advaita Vedanta.

Seymour's involvement with people becomes clear by his bringing the right coat for nearly all the guests assembled at their apartment in spite of the fact that the coats were "hung, draped, tossed, piled all over the small apartment." (92) This feat was performed when Seymour was only eight, even though he and Buddy "knew about a dozen of the guests intimately, ten or so more by sight or reputation, and the rest not at all or hardly." (92) Seymour could do it because of his innate interest in people and his instinctive love for mankind. Another instance of Seymour's desire to be in touch with the ordinary human beings is provided by his keeping in mind Miss Overman, the librarian, the representative of common man, while writing poems. Seymour felt "he owed Miss Overman a painstaking, sustained search for a form of poetry that was in accord with his own peculiar standards and yet not wholly incompatible, even at first sight, with Miss Overman's tastes." (96) Seymour's commitment to society gets further substantiated by his reluctance to offer his poems for publication. Buddy, who had found the "sheaf of poems," written by Seymour, to be "very, very good," urged him to get them published. Buddy records Seymour's response:

> No, he didn't think he could do that. Not yet; maybe never . . . . He said he felt that they were faintly affronting. He hadn't quite made up his mind where the affronting came in, but he felt at times that the poems read as though they'd been written by an ingrate, of sorts, someone who was turning his back—in effect, at least—on his own environment and the people in it who were close to him. He said he ate his food out of our big refrigerators, drove our eight-cylinder American cars, unhesitatingly used our medicines when he was sick, and relied on the U.S. Army to protect his parents and sisters from Hitler's Germany, and nothing, not one single thing in all his poems, reflected these realities. Something was terribly wrong. (95)

Seymour's involvement with his family becomes clear from his attempting and succeeding in restoring peace in the family when Waker had given away his new Davega bicycle to a poor boy, making the parents very angry.

Seymour's integrity was impeccable and he advised Buddy also to safeguard his. An "extraordinarily clear" skin and absence of any pimples on his face, even in adolescence, become symbolic of a personality with an infallible integrity. His voice was a "wholly imperfect musical instrument" and yet he never modulated his voice to deceive others, and wanted to be himself and to be seen as he really was. All these physical traits became suggestive of a straightforward, genuine, clear-hearted and flawless character. He never bothered about his clothes either. He was a careless and sloppy dresser as "once an article of clothing was actually on his body, he lost all earthly consciousness of it." (140) Not that he had no taste in choosing clothes, but just disliked getting them altered. In other words, he did not like to be a tailor-made personality and wanted to be his *real self*.

Buddy values Seymour's critical comments on his creative writings and seeks his brother's opinion about his stories. Seymour asked him once, "*Were most of your stars out: Were you busy writing your heart out?*" (120) For creative writing, complete sincerity, integrity and love have to be the cardinal principles, an important fact that Seymour teaches Buddy. Similarly, these virtues should be the tenets for living, too.

Seymour's inherent love for others got manifested in the games he played. In Buddy's words, "He used to play with the twins [his younger brothers, Walt and Waker] when they were small, and he was continually dropping hints to them to ask him if he had any fours or jacks, or elaborately coughing and exposing his hand." (145) Even at Poker, played with Buddy's friends, he would "sit there grinning" when he was "loaded with aces" like "an Easter Bunny with a whole basketful of eggs." Not only that, while holding a straight or a full check house, he would not call the opponent, who was playing only with a pair of tens, in case he liked him. In soccer and hockey also, his ways were peculiar. He would charge down-field—often brilliantly—and then stall "to give the opposing goalie time to set himself in an impregnable position." (146)

Seymour was sensitively mindful of others's feelings. Buddy recalls an incident to prove this point:

> As we were on our way to get haircuts one afternoon, he stopped dead short in the middle of Amsterdam Avenue and asked me, very soberly, with cars and trucks clipping past us from both directions, if I'd mind very much getting a haircut without him. I pulled him over to the curb (I'd like to have a nickel for every curb I pulled him over to, man and boy) and said I certainly *would* mind. He had a notion his neck wasn't clean. He was planning to spare Victor, the barber, *the offense of looking at his dirty neck*. (137, italics mine)

His younger sisters and brothers were admonished by him to take off their "rubbers on coming into the apartment," because "Bessie would have to get out the mop." (125) He was the fastest runner. Once, when they were children, he overtook Buddy, who was tearing through the streets. But he did not smirk, showing only anxiety as to why Buddy was running so fast, and thus giving no chance to the loser Buddy to feel hurt. In fact, Seymour never smirked.

IV

Buddy tries to present Seymour in true light, the essential Seymour as he came to know him. It was a difficult task, but eventually he is satisfied with his narrative. The ticklish issue of Seymour's suicide has been resolved for the reader as well as the narrator. Could Seymour, as he appears in *Raise High the Roof Beam, Carpenters; and Seymour: An Introduction* commit suicide because he was disgusted with people and sick of society? The answer is an emphatic 'No.'

Talking about Seymour brings a change in Buddy. He does not like much the creative writing class, which he teaches, because of the mediocrity of the "twenty-four young ladies,"—his students. He talks derisively of the girl-students who would be waiting, having come back "from big weekends at Cambridge or Hanover or New Haven." (156) A palpable change marks his attitude now. He realizes that "there is no single thing I do that is more important than going into that awful Room 307. There isn't one girl in there, including the Terrible Miss Zable, who is not as much my sister as Boo Boo or Franny. They may shine with the misinformation of the ages, but they shine." (157) Buddy further realizes the correctness of Seymour's vision. "Seymour once said that all we do our whole lives is go from one little piece of Holy Ground to the next." (158)

Seymour's diary and the narrative of Buddy, his brother, form the crux, the epicenter of Salinger's concept of man. This concept in the totality of the portrayal of Seymour as a character, reflects certain specific elements: transcending the ego, discerning the essence of human existence and observance of an authentic self. Feeling responsible towards the sociological environment and being willingly an inalienable part of society, form distinct characteristics of Seymour's value system.

"Hapworth 16, 1924"

"Hapworth 16, 1924" forms Salinger's last creative work in his literary career and was published in *The New Yorker* on 19 June 1965. A long letter, written by seven-year-old, clairvoyant Seymour to his family from Camp Simon Hapworth, constitutes the long story. The letter is presented verbatim by Buddy Glass, the narrator, who is now forty six, with a short introduction, explaining that the letter is another crucial step in the direction of shedding light on Seymour's personality. The letter discloses some more important facets of Seymour as a young boy who has foreknowledge of his death, at the age of thirty-one.

Seymour and his younger brother, Buddy, who is five, are staying at Camp Simon Hapworth for the summer. The camp is run by Mr. and Mrs. Happy whose married life is far from happy. The atmosphere at the Camp is degenerate and perverse. Seymour's letter describes the world of "Hapworth." It also contains advice to his parents and exhortations to his younger brothers and sisters for an integrated development of their personality, while simultaneously unravelling Seymour's own character.

This long story marks a climactic formulation of Salinger's vision of man, besides containing a searching scrutiny of man's plight in a repellent world. The novelist's philosophic thrust is directed towards a clear and emphatic assertion of the values considered essential for the ideal man. Through the young protagonist, the novelist categorically rejects escape from society on account of the prevalent perversions, promiscuity and moral decadence. Consciousness of the baneful in society, and the efforts to confront and come to grips with it through compassion and generosity, become some of the crucial and potent values. The foreknowledge of death neither depresses the eight-year-old protagonist into inertia and alienation, nor does it discourage him into abandoning the values of love, contact, communication and responsibility, observed by him in his daily life.

Seymour as a boy possesses the same personality-traits as witnessed in the older Seymour of the other works. The precocious, sensitive and intelligent Seymour believes in consciously working on his weaknesses. It is only natural that a grown up, saintly Seymour should have had a childhood in which, besides his precocious intelligence and sensitivity, he is shown to cherish spiritual values. Aware of his previous births, as also about his present life-span, the young Seymour says: "There is monumental work to be done" adding "My time is too limited, quite to my sadness and amusement." (Salinger 1965:36) Seymour's generously affectionate concern for the most ordinary people gets revealed in his attitude towards the spinster librarian, Miss Overman. She is vain and conservative and has little touch with reality. He tells his parents that Miss Overman may be archaic in her beliefs but she is simple-hearted and should not be regarded by them as a "fuddy duddy" because she is not one. He remarks, "In her disarming modest way, that little bit of a woman has quite a lot of the simplicity and dear fortitude of an unrecorded heroine of the Civil or Crimean War, perhaps the most moving wars of the last few centuries. My God, please take the slight trouble to remember that this worthy woman and spinster has no comfortable home in the present century!" (32-33) Not only that; he does not want to deprive Miss Overman the egoistic pleasure of dissecting and criticizing his penmanship. Like Miss Overman, Wilfred G.L. Fraser, at the Library Council, is also a vain and egoistic person. But Seymour's attitude towards Mr. Fraser also is not unpleasant.

II

Life at Camp Hapworth, Maine, where the two brothers, Seymour and Buddy, have gone to spend the summer, is a microcosm of the squalid reality in the post-Second World War America. "Pale sunshine" streams through a "filthy window" of the room in which the two youngsters have been put up. The food served to the campers is "not atrocious" but "is cooked without a morsel of affection or inspiration, each string bean and simple carrot arriving on the Camper's plate quite stripped of its tiny vegetal soul." (33) The reason for this is that the cooks, Mr. and Mrs. Nelson, cannot bring themselves to "imagine that every boy who comes into their mess hall is their own beloved child, regardless of from whose loins he sprang in this particular appearance." (33) Consequently, "a nameless inertia hangs over those two alternating with fits of unreasonable wrath, stripping them of any will or desire to prepare creditable, affectionate food or even to keep the bent silverware on the tables spotless and clean as a whistle." (33)

The Camp, besides being full of physical uncleanliness, abounds in moral squalor. Homosexuality is practised among the senior campers. Sensuality is rampant. Both, the counsellors and the senior campers, have been scheming to have sex with Miss Culgerry, who is a nurse at the Camp-infirmary. She is a silly and confused woman with a "superb body," having either already lost her virginity or in imminent danger of losing it.

The majority of the young campers are riven with suspicion, cliquism and a craze for "popularity" or "dubious prestige." An appalling lack of original thinking makes Seymour lament: "Unfortunately here as elsewhere on this touching planet, imitation is the watchword and prestige the highest ambition." (34) There is hardly any likelihood of the majority among the boys at the Camp ever attaining maturity, and most of them "will merely senesce." Griffith Hammersmith, one of the campers, has a severe speech impediment and has "to sleep with a rubber sheet on his bed," (34) besides being absolutely averse to brushing his teeth. Mrs. Hammersmith, his mother, is "a young divorcee with an exquisite, swanky face slightly ravaged by vanity and self-love and a few silly disappointments in life, though not silly to her." (34) Salinger lambasts the bourgeois value-orientation by revealing Mrs. Hammersmith's mentality in preferring rich friends for her son rather than intelligent and sensitive boys like Seymour and Buddy. Her falseness, hypocrisy and a mistaken sense of superiority, resulting from her "great monetary wealth" become symbolic of the malaise afflicting the contemporary American society.

The counsellors at the Camp are actually pseudo-counsellors, being hardly in a position to offer any sound guidance, as they themselves are narrow-minded, unenlightened bigots. Whitey Pitman, the head counsellor, is insensitive, mean and egoistic who, at best, can be described as an "intelligent scavenger," since he does not hesitate to increase "his own prestige at some child's expenses." (42) Indifference and stupidity become the counsellors's characteristic qualities. With such counsellors, the fate of the Camp may well be imagined.

Mr. and Mrs. Happy, who run the Camp, have a "rotten married life." Theirs is not the only soured marriage; the Camp proliferates with "rotten marriages." Mrs. Happy, a figure of intense sensuality, with "her perfect legs, ankles, saucy bosom, very fresh cute hindquarters" (35) is a liar besides being a shallow and confused person. She is "growing prepared to make delirious love to an attractive stranger," (38) who has come to visit the Camp. He is a "war buddy" of Mr. Happy, and is now a Congressman. Mrs. Happy is a silly, chattering individual who must confide her personal problems in somebody—even though he be a child of seven.

Indifference, obsequiousness and artificiality are the hallmarks of Mr. Happy. During the visit of the United States Congressman, Mr. Happy turns into a sycophant. The streak of cruelty in him is revealed in his rough treatment of children and using two horses instead of four, the required number, for pulling a cart. He has no sense of human kinship with anyone, including his wife.

Finding himself in this moral and physical squalor, Seymour's response is not despair and withdrawal. No doubt, sometimes he feels enraged and sad at what he encounters. The stupidities and the heartless indifference of the counsellors at the Camp make him secretly wish that he "could improve matters quite substantially by bashing a few culprits over the head with an excellent shovel or stout club." (34) He also feels enraged at Whitey Pitman, the head counsellor, who tells Buddy in the midst of a throng of strangers: "I thought you were supposed to be such a witty kid." (44) He threatens Mr. Pitman that he would kill him or himself "possibly before nightfall, if he spoke to this chap again in that matter or any other five-year-old chap." (44) The bourgeois mentality of social pride in Mrs. Hammersmith is found "inexcusable and hopeless" by Seymour. It saddens Seymour that "friendship in this world is being corrupted by countless strings attached and personal interests." (88) Certain books give rise in him to "shame and anger" as do the books *Alexander* by Alfred Erdonna and *Origins and Speculations* by Theo Acton Baum. Alfred Erdonna, in a biography of Alexander the Great sounds smug and superior even to Alexander which irritates Seymour. Theo Acton Baum's book is "dubious and very dangerous, untalented, a cold hearted work of literature." (103) But as Seymour puts on record on more than one occasion, he is conscious of his anger, malice and contempt for some people, and not approving of such flaws in his character, tries to get rid of these. He admits that "a vein of instability runs through me quite like some turbulent river"; and rues that "I have left this troublesome instability uncorrected in my previous two appearances, to my folly and disgust." (44) His unflinching belief in self-reliant action gets revealed in his resolve about overcoming this flaw: "it will not be corrected by a friendly, cheerful prayer. It can only be corrected by dogged effort on my part, thank God. I cannot honorably or intimately pray to some charming, divine weakling to step in and clean my mess up after me; the very prospect turns my stomach." (67) As Seymour feels that he can correct it by dogged effort on his part, his frequent refrain is "I am working on it," (67) which shows his desire to improve himself.

Seymour is also conscious of his several other weaknesses. For example, he is fully conscious of his and Buddy's being "sensualists from the word go" but asserts that neither he nor Buddy has "the slightest intention of dying by the phallus as surely as the sword; we fully intend to come to grips with the subject of sensuality." (96) Seymour goes on to declare, "I for one do not look forward to being distracted by charming lusts of the body, quite day in and day out, for the few, blissful, remaining years allotted to me in this appearance." (36) The young Seymour knows that his opinions about other people at times "are all too frequently too damn harsh for words" and confesses that he has "given way to harshness too often this summer to stomach." (52) However, Seymour is "working on" this weakness, too.

III

Surrounded by a squalid reality as Seymour is, he does not

detach himself from society as becomes clear from his words: "it is not in your son Buddy's nature or mine or your son Walter's to be in the least shocked or disgusted by any sweet, earthly side of humankind. Indeed, all forms of human folly and bestiality touch a very sympathetic chord within our breasts." (36) In the midst of "black and quite dank side of camp life," Seymour does not fail to find "the countless things that are zipping along with smoothness and beauty." (49) He records that "each day has been generously studded with happiness, sensuous pleasure, rejoicing, and fairly explosive laughter. Many sweet animals loom into view when least expected." (56) There are so many joys, consolations, and amusing compensations that Seymour's and Buddy's lives "remain an unforgettable waltz." (56) Seymour's capacity to see beauty amidst moral stench is in conformity with his ability to discern "the main current of poetry that flows through things, all things." (57) when he grows older. Therefore, there is willing participation on Seymour's part (as well as Buddy's) in Camp life which comes out in his remark: "We are mixing admirably when opportunity allows, joining in all incessant sports and other activities, enjoying many of them to the hilt." (55) The young perceptive hero celebrates being a part of society when he writes:

> In addition to distant music, adventure and romance press us hard; absorbing interests and diversions kindly prevail; not once have I seen us unprotected, thank God, against half-heartedness. One has no business spitting at these hopeful blessings. Piled on top of all this good fortune, what else does one find? A capacity to make wonderful friends in small numbers whom we will love passionately and guard from uninstructive harm until our lives are finished and who, in turn will love us, too, and never let us down without any great regret. (56-58)

This constitutes an emphatic rebuttal of Richard H. Rupp's stance that Seymour's asking for a large number of books for reading at the Camp becomes his act of escape inasmuch as the world of books constitutes "a substitute world" for the "real world" and that "having rejected human society with its multiple ills, Seymour projects a wholly illusory world of fictive creatures." (1970:130) Not only does Seymour accept the world with all its ills, but also feels a sense of responsibility towards it. Seymour is basically a humanist, pitying mankind but not hating it. The crudities, deformities and the filth he encounters around him make him more and more sad, but never for a moment does he detest humanity. His every effort is directed towards striking a healthy bond of interaction and inter-relationships with other human beings. His humanism gets further illustrated by his feeling apprehensive and worried on account of Mrs. Happy who is on the verge of committing adultery. The young protagonist's sense of keen responsibility and eagerness to involve himself with humanity gets further reflected because no reason is considered valid by him "to excuse myself from keen responsibility because I am a mere boy of seven. If I excuse myself on such flimsy, rotten grounds, then I am a liar or a cowardly fraud and maker of cheap, normal excuses." (38) Seymour's selfless love reveals itself in his remark: "It is entirely disgusting to be for ever achieving little actions of the heart or body and then taking recourse to reaction. I am utterly convinced that if A's hat blows off while he is sauntering down the street, it is the charming duty of B to pick it up and hand it to A without examining A's face or combing it for gratitude!" (32) The young hero is fully committed to his social responsibility: "With just a little steadfast devotion to uncommon beauty and passing rectitudes of the heart, combined with our dead certainty that we are as normal and human as anybody else, and it is not just a question of sticking out our tongues, like other boys, during the first, beautiful snowfall of the year, who can prevent us from doing a little good in this appearance? Who, indeed, I say, provided we draw on all our resources." (58-60) The young boy is cognizant of every little detail in the surrounding reality. In the words of Alfred Kazin, "To notice every seeming triviality (Seymour protests that he loves, loves, loves, everything and everyone in his path) is to respect the creation—and gives Salinger's fiction its dense social structure." (1973:118) Alfred Kazin's words epitomize Salinger's eager concern for sociological upliftment and a productive involvement of an individual with society, symbolized by Seymour's sensitive response to happenings at the Camp.

Seymour represents the ideal that is eventually cherished by the other members of the Glass family in order to live and survive in a loveless world, full of crudity, and vulgarity. He stands for rigorous standards of perfection in sincerity: "I am sick to death of the wide gap of embarrassing differences among other things, between my writing and speaking voices! It is rotten and worrisome to have two voices." (32) His belief in the invincible and inexhaustible resources within human beings is firm and intense and this makes him assert that in any crisis "the jig is never damnable and never up; when it maddeningly appears to be, it is merely time to rally one's magnificent forces again and review the issue." (94) He prizes self-knowledge and self-improvement and blames himself and Buddy for the antagonism that others feel towards them: "I am hoping," he writes, "however, that as we continue to improve and refine our characters by leaps and bounds striving each day to reduce general snottiness, surface conceits, and too damn much emotion, coupled with several other qualities quite rotten to the core, we will antagonize and inspire less murder, on sight or repute alone, in the hearts of fellow beings." (56) Seymour's refusal to undergo anesthesia, when he gets injured and the wound has to be stitched at the infirmary, shows his love for consciousness and preparedness to suffer pain in life. He puts it on record, "I prefer not to allow myself or any other child in the family to give up his or her state of consciousness for flimsy reasons; until I get further word on the subject, the human state of consciousness is dubiously precious to me." (73)

The young hero advises his mother "to sing in your own abandoned voice when making 'Bambalina' with Les!" (78) He even becomes an unsparing critic of his own father, Les, who is a singer, by telling the latter that his Australian accent is no longer "delectable, quite possibly to anybody" and, therefore, he should try to keep it out while singing for making of a record, in case he wants to make "a smash hit finally." (80) Boo Boo, his younger sister, is also advised by him to practise "writing of complete words!" and not to "fall back on conventional excuses" (80) of her tender age. Any other child of her acquaintance and her age "is not required to read and write quite fluently." (80) Seymour also wants her to improve her manners and etiquette and be absolutely sincere: "I am far less concerned about how you behave in public than how you behave when you are absolutely alone in a solitary room. When you accidentally look deep into a long mirror, let a girl with stunning tact, as well as flashing black eyes, reflect." (80) He tells her without mincing words that her preference for "ritzy things," books "with well-bred, aristocratic, uncrude children and adults in them, usually English persons with excellent manners on the surface, tasteful clothes and interiors, as well as unassailably high class in every visible respect," (85) might make her a superficial and artificial person, a show off. She is warned: "if you grew up and knew in your heart that your excellent, ritzy manners in public were merely skin deep, leaving you free to be quite a dirty pig when alone in a room with no one watching but yourself, you would be far from pleased; it would quite corrode you, in a subtle manner." (85) In a vainglorious society, he wants Boo Boo to be humble and pray every night before going to bed, even if she has objections to using the word God in the prayer. Walt, his three-year-old brother, is also advised to continuously practise dancing, and the other brother, Waker, to practise juggling regularly, if they have not given up their chosen careers. Seymour's desire to communicate and his prizing "communication" become clear from his revealing words: "Ye gods and little fishes! How cheerful and rewarding it is to have a little leisure for communication with one's family during one's busy camp life! You can easily fail to suspect how damn much blessed time I have on my hands today to attend to the needs of the heart." (36-37) All this again stoutly contradicts the charge of escapism levelled on Seymour by some critics.

Salinger holds that "truth" and "love" are values which need to be pursued relentlessly even in a world (as revealed in "Hapworth") in which superciliousness and hypocrisy are rampant. Seymour writes:

> Every man, woman, and child over the age let us say, of twenty one or thirty at the very outside, should never do anything without first consulting a list of persons in the world, living or dead, whom he loves. Remember, I implore you, that he has no right whatever to include on this list anybody

> he merely admires quite to distraction! If the person or persons' contributions have not roused his love, and unexplainable happiness or eternal warmth, that person must be ruthlessly severed from the list. My God, it could be the finest, most terrible, personal guard against deceit and lies both to oneself and to any friends or acquaintances in casual or heated conversation with oneself. (98-100)

Young Seymour admits that he does not know where such a practice will lead one to, but stresses "if it does not lead to more lies in the world, it is something." (100)

Rupp is again wrong in his interpretation of "Hapworth" when he says, "'Hapworth' even lacks the Fat Lady, Salinger's acknowledgement of the human ills. There is no Fat Lady in Seymour's world. Indeed, there never was—only an avowed love for man in the abstract, a love much like Gulliver's love of rationality. . . . In the Glass world, Salinger has rejected the pain, vices, and absurdities of ordinary human life for the Land of the Houyhnhnms (nee Glass). Seymour returns to us from his spiritual voyages, a jovial Gulliver, i.e., a monster." (1970:130) Calling Seymour a "monster" who returns from his "spiritual voyages" constitutes a blatant travesty of the message that Salinger conveys through the portrayal of his young protagonist. Far from rejecting the "pain, vices, and absurdities of ordinary human life," the author makes Seymour grapple with these social ills with sincerity and application, besides making him improve the degree of his consciousness. Seymour's own words in this context provide a forceful contradiction to Rupp's contention. Referring to himself and his brothers and sisters, he writes that most of them "have a fairly terrible capacity for experiencing pain that does not always properly belong to them." (60) There are other people who have either shirked their share of pain or "did not know how to grasp it firmly by the handle!" (60) But Seymour tells his parents, "Speaking for your absent son Buddy as well as myself, I see no way to quit experiencing a little pain here and there, till we have fulfilled our opportunities and obligations in the present, interesting, humorous bodies. . . . However, when we have fulfilled our opportunities and obligations, dear Bessie and Les, I give you my word that we will depart in good conscience and humor for a change, which we have never done in the past." (60) An incontrovertible proof of Seymour's extra-ordinarily alive and receptive mind, a mind and a psyche that always reverberate with empathy, compassion and Christian love, comes in the form of the long letter. The letter which Seymour writes not only becomes a document of personality-revelation, but symbolizes as well, a declaration in certain essential humanistic values, ideas and precepts which according to Salinger play a major role in making an individual exceptionally moral and socially responsible in a world largely dominated by repulsive, abhorrent and despicable tendencies.

"Hapworth," thus, becomes a decisive rebuttal to such unfounded criticism as "The Glasses respond by a progressive withdrawal from reality." (Rupp 1970: 131) and an unmincing answer to unperceptive observations like Seymour's "loving absorption of all life became nihilistic for him in his suicide." (Schulz 1969: 212)

Conclusion

Right from the beginning of his literary career, a dominant concern for J.D. Salinger has been man's predicament in society and finding a solution to it. This concern reflects itself in the novelist's delineation of the modern American protagonist as an individual in action, operating as a secular Adam. This Adamic figure operates largely in a demonic human world where the only panacea becomes consciousness, willing, living and assuming responsibility. The philosophy of "Karma" (Action) and reincarnation as enshrined in Advaita Vedanta acts as a motivating force in assumption of responsibility by the protagonists. Other religious tenets which enable man to live a conscious and meaningful life are derived from Christian thought, Taoism and Zen Buddhism. Christianity makes them serve Christ by serving the humble and suffering humanity. Taoism teaches them to reach the essence of things and discern beauty amidst moral squalor. Zen Buddhism makes them cherish egolessness. Religion, however, remains a tool for Salinger's protagonists in the quest for a solution to their predicament vis-a-vis society.

Salinger's works reveal an organic growth of his concept of man. The early stories reveal a groping for some viable solution to man's existential despair. *The Catcher in the Rye* and *Nine Stories*—works of intervening period—reflect the formulation of his concept of man, howsoever tentative. The protagonists in these works embody the need to cherish a dream and the desirability of infusing love in human relationships. The later works like *Raise High the Roof Beam, Carpenters; and Seymour: An Introduction* and "Hapworth 16, 1924" constitute a decisive testament of acceptance of society and assumption of social responsibility. Simultaneously, the novelist's concept of man may be seen operating within the individual works, too.

In his early stories, Salinger is not yet clear about the values he wants his protagonists to cherish and practise. Consequently, they are unable to grapple with the castrating and destructive forces at work. Some of them capitulate to the prevailing corruption and degenerate into animality. Some others succumb to these forces and end up alienated, defeated or destroyed.

The forces that assault man and shatter his spirit are diverse. They are embodied in an autocratic mother, Mrs. Evelyn Cooney ("Elaine") and selfish, corrupt and nasty mistress, Mary Gates Croft ("The Inverted Forest"). The protagonists of these two stories find comfort either in the unreal world of movies or the world of imagination. War is delineated as a hydra-headed monster. It bludgeons the youth into not marching out of step, nipping the spirit of non-conformity in the bud. It causes loss, despair and depression, killing the good and the kind-hearted. The war strains human relationships. The survivors become drained out of their emotional resources. Having experienced the ravages of war, the protagonists become incapable of entering into fresh relationships ("The Hang of It," "A Boy in France," "Last Day of the Last Furlough"). Mammon presides over an acquisitive society. Mercinariness shatters the aesthetic dream ("The Varioni Brothers"). Pervasive phoniness and chasing of material success bring about gloomy and despairing alienation ("Slight Rebellion off Madison").

By the time Salinger wrote *The Catcher in the Rye* (several stories were written simultaneously with this novel), he had formulated, somewhat tentatively, his concept of man. In this novel, he invests the protagonist with those values which according to him are crucial in confronting the dystopian world of contemporary America. Salinger's ideal man is aware of his self as well as the surrounding reality. The fake and the phonies fill him with disgust and depression, but only temporarily. The "Fuck Yous" scrawled all around, sexual perversions and distorted values alienate him, precipitating feelings of flight and nervous breakdown. But the protagonist's innate love and assumption of responsibility act as redemptive forces.

The major protagonists in *Nine Stories* epitomize values which can redeem man in his sociological predicament. These values, in fact, form the constituents of the novelist's concept of man. Mysticism and excessive spirituality are rejected for their alienating tendencies. Seymour's suicide in "A Perfect Day for Bananafish" is made to serve as a strident denunciation of excessive spirituality. Capitulation to corruption inevitably leads to dehumanization of the self, filling life with mounting frustration and rancid bitterness. The net result of these is either masochism or sadism as it happens to Eloise ("Uncle Wiggily in Connecticut"). Self-awareness is considered as a prime requisite for redemption. Those who have this faculty possess the potential for ending their isolation and stemming their moral rot. Even among children, self-awareness is to be encouraged ("Down at the Dinghy"). Love saves human relationships in the process of falling asunder. Franklin's affectionate concern for Ginnie Mannox restores friendly feelings between Ginnie Mannox and Selena ("Just Before the War with the Eskimos"). Love also acts as a redeeming force, with curative powers; it can bring man out of his despair and nervous breakdown ("For Esme—With Love and Squalor"). Refusal to shoulder responsibilities which love demands causes unhappiness to all concerned ("The Laughing Man"). There is no room for sexual promiscuity for Salinger's ideal man. Dignity of the self is to be prized and can be asserted even in the face of a bitchy wife and a treacherous superior and friend. Lee's remorse ("Pretty Mouth and Green My Eyes") at his own debauchery and betrayal of his friend and subordinate, Arthur, constitutes Salinger's condemnation of sexual immorality. The falling of cigarette-ash on Lee's chest becomes the fire and brimstone imagery vis-a-vis the adulterer. In "De Daumier-Smith's Blue Period" and "Teddy," Salinger treats human relationships as sacrosanct. Involvement with, and commitment to society, even in the face of foreknowledge of an early death, are the moral obligations of man.

Salinger becomes sure of his stance in *Franny and Zooey*. No reason is regarded as potent enough for escaping the reality—not even religion and mysticism. Franny's withdrawal from an egocentric, hedonistic, sham society, into the religious retreat of her Jesus Prayer gets roundly denounced by Zooey as an act of escape and selfish acquisitiveness. The Vedantic tenet of "Karma" (action) is regarded as the guiding force of human existence. The theory of reincarnation is used to emphasize one's obligation to one's

"Karma" (action) irrespective of one's predilection for or against the work one happens to be doing. Simultaneously, the Christian precept of serving Christ through the service of the suffering humanity is preached. The parable of the "Fat Lady" equates the suffering Fat Lady with Christ. Seymour's advice to Franny to be funny and to Zooey to shine his shoes for the Fat Lady before going to the Radio programme, 'It's a Wise Child,' embodies the principle not only of acceptance of society but also of assumption of social responsibility. Franny comes out of her nervous breakdown and becomes happy. Zooey's relationship with society no longer remains uneasy once he perceives the true meaning of Seymour's advice, which he imparts to Franny as well.

Salinger's concept of man acquires decisiveness in *Raise High the Roof Beam, Carpenters; and Seymour: An Introduction* and "Hapworth 16, 1924." These works explicate Seymour's personality who, by and large, epitomizes Salinger's ideal of man. Seymour's suicide emerges not as an act of disgust with society, but as the result of his inability to end his alienation. Seymour embodies the Taoist theory of essence which enables him to discern beauty in the routine, drab and vulgar society. His innate love, compassion, humility, integrity project him as a saint, incapable of hatred. Through him, Salinger highlights the sanctity of all human activity and emphasizes the need to assume social responsibility. Seymour's perception of life is that "all we do our whole lives is go from one little piece of Holy Ground to the next."

"Hapworth 16, 1924" emphatically underscores certain virtues which form elements of Salinger's concept of man. Sexual restraint is to be practised even in the face of seductive charms. "Consciousness" is valuable. Truthfulness is to be cherished. Deceit and hypocrisy are to be discarded. Contact with and considerateness towards the most ordinary and the crass is called for. Moral improvement of the self is desirable. Involvement with society and assumption of social responsibility are to be maintained unflinchingly in the face of foreknowledge of death at a particular time. Death is to be treated as nothing more than a landmark in the cycle of reincarnations of the soul.

The dystopian reality causes despair, depression and alienation. But Salinger's contention is that it is within man's power to dispel despair and attain hope, overcome his alienation and assume responsibility. Therefore, Salinger's major protagonists seem to embark on a journey from melancholia and despair to joy and hope, from innocence and *insouciance* to maturity and acceptance of reality and assumption of social responsibility. The typical Salinger protagonist manages to preserve the integrity and dignity of his self while successfully grappling with the life-denying forces. His sensibility, sharpened by his conscious existence, enables him to discern a great contrast between beauty, dream, love and spiritual maximalism on the one hand and, what Holden calls "phoney," on the other. Religion becomes instrumental in evolving a mode of living for man caught in his sociological predicament; whereas religion, or mysticism as a source of escape from reality gets categorically rejected.

The novelist's stance vis-a-vis the absurd or hostile environment conforms to the recognizable humanistic tradition, according to which mankind can still nourish hope for a better future. In spite of a demonic or dystopian environment, the individual self can work out its resurgence, thus keeping human values. Salinger's concept of man or the self in relation to the post-Second World War sociological environment is quite different from the concept of the self contained in angry, pessimistic, even nihilistic literature of the same era. There is an emphatic and unequivocal repudiation of the concept of the self seeking refuge in sex, violence, masochism, sadism and even religion or mysticism. While the protagonists of Salinger's contemporaries like John Updike, William Styron and Saul Bellow fight despair and affirm hope, Salinger's fictional personages mark an advance in this direction. They not only cherish but also try to practise positive objectives for the attainment of healthy and desirable values which alone can evolve and sustain hope and optimism for the betterment of humanity. In this respect, the typical Salinger protagonist embodies a metaphoric and even metaphysical resurrection of the self while keeping the individual being firmly anchored to the sociological milieu. As a secular Adam, the Salinger hero finally succeeds in attaining a realistic solution in the form of an acceptance of the role to be played by the self in a dystopian social reality. The protagonists of the later works assume more social responsibility and reject any type of elusive, escapist or unrealistic attitude which would alienate the individual from the sociological environment in which every human being has to operate. Assumption of a practical role in society gets invested with sacred or religious dimensions. Performing a social role becomes a type of religious worship, and the more the Salinger hero gets involved in social interaction, the more spiritual satisfaction he experiences. Thus, it can be safely said that unlike most of the modernist protagonists of contemporary American fiction, the people who inhabit the fictional world of Salinger's novels do not desist from playing their social roles in a positive manner, after the initial doubts and hesitancy have been overcome. The concept of man as an individual performing in a phoney, degenerate and debased society, passes through two crucial phases. Confrontation with such a society does at first breed disgust, despair, despondency and even alienation—institutionalized and conventional religion adding to the isolation of the individual self. But eventually, religious tenets become a positive instrument in overcoming despair and alienation and not only integrating the individual self with society but making him take up social responsibility. Thus, Salinger's concept of man becomes quintessentially socio-religious in which the novelist accomplishes a strategic amalgam of the sociological and the religious approaches to arrive at a kind of hybrid concept, making limited use of certain religious tenets as a kind of launching pad for a constantly evolving concept of man from the early to the later works.

In his eagerness to delineate his concept of man in no uncertain terms, Salinger adopts a well thought out strategy. He kills Seymour—his chief protagonist of several works—in one of the early stories. In the later works, the novelist proceeds with dexterous artistry to recreate and rebuild all those circumstances and reasons responsible for his hero's tragic end. This enables the novelist to construct a corpus of investigation on which he slowly but surely goes to delineate his concept of man. In doing so, a visibly perceptive change comes in the form and the structure of the later works when it becomes clear that the thematic interest triumphs over the fictional interest. In other words the ordinary novelistic requirements of plot, characterization, theme and imagery are treated in an almost unconventional manner. It only shows the firm commitment of a highly conscious creative artist to make his narrative matrix a powerful instrument for conveying an important message. The message in this case is the same concept of man as it emerges in the totality of the works studied.

Salinger's concept of man evolves finally into the idea of an individual operating or functioning in a dystopian world, a being who seeks the use and acceptance of religious tenets for individual resurgence and yet does not use religion and religious mysticism as a means of escape from social responsibility. The Salinger hero, finally, accepts his role in society willingly and in the process utilizes religion as a catalytic force to propel the individual self towards the final objective: willing acceptance of responsibility and a healthy role in society.

Works Cited

Primary Sources

Salinger, J.D. 1958. (First published 1951). *The Catcher in the Rye*. Harmondsworth, Middlesex, England: Penguin.

________. 1964 (First published 1953). *Nine Stories*. New York: Bantam. ("A Perfect Day for Bananafish," "Uncle Wiggily in Connecticut," "Just Before the War with the Eskimos," "The Laughing Man," "Down at the Dinghy," "For Esme—With Love and Squalor," "Pretty Mouth and Green My Eyes," "De Daumier-Smith's Blue Period," "Teddy.")

________.1964a. (First published 1961). *Franny and Zooey*. Harmondsworth, Middlesex, England: Penguin.

________. 1964b. (First published 1963). *Raise High the Roof Beam, Carpenters; and Seymour: An Introduction*. Harmondsworth, Middlesex, England: Penguin.

________. 1938. "Musings of a Social Soph: The Skipped Diploma." *Ursinus Weekly* (10 October) 2.

________. 1940. "The Young Folks." *Story*, 16 (March-April): 26-30.

________. 1940a. "Go See Eddie." *The University of Kansas City Review*, 7 (December): 121-24.

________. 1941. "The Hang of It." *Collier's*. (12 July): 22.

________. 1941a. "The Heart of a Broken Story." *Esquire* 16 (September): 32, 131-33.

________. 1942. "The Long Debut of Louis Tagget." *Story* 21 (September-October): 28-34.

________. 1942a. "Personal Notes on an Infantryman." *Collier's* (12 December), 96.

________. 1943. "The Varioni Brothers." *The Saturday Evening Post* (17 July): 12-13, 76-77.

________. 1944 "Both Parties Concerned." *The Saturday Evening Post* (26 February): 14, 47-48.

________. 1944a. "Soft-Boiled Sergeant." *The Saturday Evening Post* (15 April): 18, 82, 84-85.

________. 1944b. "Last Day of the Last Furlough." *The Saturday Evening Post* (15 July): 26-27, 61-62, 64.

________. 1944c. "Once a Week Won't Kill You." *Story*, 25 (November-December): 23-27.

________. 1945. "A Boy in France." *The Saturday Evening Post* (31 March): 21, 92.

________. 1945a. "Elaine." *Story* 26 (March-April): 38-47.

________. 1945b. "This Sandwich Has No Mayonnaise." *Esquire* 24 (October): 54-56, 147-49.

________. 1945c. "The Stranger." *Collier's* (1 December): 18, 77.

________. 1945d. "I'm Crazy." *Collier's* (22 December): 36, 48, 51.

________. 1946. "Slight Rebellion off Madison." *The New Yorker* (21 December): 76-79.

________. 1947. "A Young Girl in 1941 with No Waist at All." *Mademoiselle* 25 (May): 222-23, 292-302.

________. 1947a. "The Inverted Forest." *Cosmopolitan* 123 (December): 73-80, 85-86, 88, 90, 92, 95-96, 98, 100, 102, 107, 109.

________. 1948. "A Girl I Knew." *Good Housekeeping* 126 (February): 37, 186, 188, 191-96.

________. 1948a. "Blue Melody." *Cosmopolitan* 125 (September): 51, 112-19.

________. 1965. "Hapworth 16, 1924." *The New Yorker* (19 June): 32-113.

Secondary Sources

Alsen, Eberhard. 1980. "'Raise High the Roof Beam, Carpenters' and the Amateur Reader." *Studies in Short Fiction* 17: 1: 39-47.

________. 1983. *Salinger's Glass Stories as a Composite Novel*. Troy, New York: The Whitston.

Antico, Eugene Dale. 1991. Ph.D. Thesis. *The Fiction of J.D. Salinger: A Search through Taoism*. The Florida State University.

Antico, John. 1966. "The Parody of J.D. Salinger's Esme and the Fat Lady Exposed." *Modern Fiction Studies*. 12: 325-40.

Balbert, Peter. 1980. "Configurations of the Ego: Studies of Mailer, Roth and Salinger." (Review Article). *Studies in the Novel*, 12: 1: 73-81.

Barr, Donald. 1964. "J.D. Salinger: Saints, Pilgrims and Artists." in Richard Kostelanetz. 538.41.

Barrett, William. 1969. "American Fiction and Values." In Marcus Klein.

Baskett, Sam S. 1963. "The Splendid Squalid World of J.D. Salinger." *Wisconsin Studies in Contemporary Literature* 4: 1: 48-61.

Baumbach, Jonathan. 1965: *The Landscape of Nightmare: Studies in the Contemporary American Novel*. New York: New York University Press.

Belcher, William F. and James W. Lee, ed. 1962. *J.D. Salinger and the Critics*. Belmont, California: Wadsworth.

Blaney, Shirlie. 1963 "Twin State Telescope." In Warren French.

Boe, Alfred F. 1987. "Street Games in J.D. Salinger and Gerald Green." *Modern Fiction Studies* 33: 65-72.

Bowden, Edwin T. 1961. *The Dungeon of the Heart: Human Isolation and the American Novel*. New York: The Macmillan.

Branch, Edgar. 1963. "Mark Twain and J.D. Salinger: A Study in Literary Continuity." In Herold P. Simonson and Philip E. Hager.

Broes, Arthur T., ed. 1963. *Lectures on Modern Novelists*. Pittsburgh: Carnegie Institute of Technology.

Brookman, Christopher. 1991. "Pencey Preppy: Cultural Codes in *The Catcher in the Rye*." In Jack Salzman.

Bryant, Jerry H. 1970. *The Open Decision: The Contemporary American Novel and Its Intellectual Background*. New York: The Free Press.

Bungert, Hans. 1963. "Salinger's *The Catcher in the Rye:* "Isolated Youth and His Struggle to Communicate." In Marvin Laser and Norman Fruman.

Camus, Albert. 1975. *The Myth of Sisyphus*. Harmondsworth, Middlesex: Penguin.

________. 1975a. *The Rebel*. Harmondsworth, Middlesex: Penguin.

Chester, Alfred. 1963. "Salinger: How to Love Without Love." *Commentary*, 35: 6 (June): 467-74.

Cohen, Hubert I. 1966, "'A Woeful Agony which Forced Me to Begin My Tale': *The Catcher in the Rye*." *Modern Fiction Studies* 12 (Special Number): 355-66.

Dalbanco, Andrew. 1987. "Holden Caulfield Goes to Law School." *The New Republic* (9 March): 27.

Davis, Tom. 1963. "J.D. Salinger: 'The Sound of One Hand Clapping." *Wisconsin Studies in Contemporary Literature*, 4:1: 41-47.

________. 1963. J.D. Salinger: A Checklist. In Warren French.

De Mott, Benjamin. 1965. "Dirty Words?" *The Hudson Review* 18: 1:31-44.

Edwards, Duane. 1977. "Holden Caulfield: 'Don't Ever Tell Anybody Anything.'" *ELH* 44: 554-65.

Elfin, Mel. 1960. "The Mysterious J.D. Salinger . . . His Woodsy, Secluded Life." *Newsweek* (30 May), 92-94.

Eliade, Mercea. 1965. "The Sacred and the Modern Artist." *Criterion* 4:2.

Eppes, Betty. 1981. "What I Did Last Summer." *The Paris Review* 23.80: 221-39.

Fiedler, Leslie A. 1962. "The Eye of Innocence" (abridged), in Henry Anatole Grunwald.

Field, Michele. 1986. "In Pursuit of J.D. Salinger." *Publishers Weekly* (27 June), 63-64.

Finkelstein, Sidney. 1968. *Existentialism and Alienation in American Literature*. New York: International Publishers.

Foley, Martha, ed. 1949. "Salinger, J.D." in *The Best American Short Stories of 1949: and the Yearbook of the American Short Story*. Boston: Houghton Mifflin.

French, Warren. 1963. *J.D. Salinger*. New York: Twayne.

_______. 1965. "An Unnoticed Salinger Story." *College English* 26 (February): 394-95.

_______. 1963. "The Phony World and the Nice World." *Wisconsin Studies in Contemporary Literature* 4:1:21-30.

_______. 1964-65. "Holden's Fall." *Modern Fiction Studies* 10:389.

_______, ed. 1970. "The Age of Salinger." *The Fifties: Fiction, Poetry, Drama*. De Land, Florida: Everett/Edwards, 25-38.

_______. 1973. "Steinbeck and J.D. Salinger." *Steinbeck's Literary Dimensions: A Guide to Comparative Studies*. Metuchen, New Jersey: Scarecrow, 105-15.

Fry, Northrop. 1957. *Anatomy of Criticism*. Princeton: Princeton University Press.

Galloway, David D. 1981. *The Absurd Hero in American Fiction: Updike, Styron, Bellow, Salinger*. Austin: University of Texas Press.

Geismar, Maxwell. 1958. *American Moderns: From Rebellion to Conformity*. New York: Hill and Wang.

Ghose, Sisir Kumar. 1965. "Sorrows of J.D. Salinger." *Quest* 46 (July/September): 48-53.

Goad, Angela Lee. 1995. M.A. Thesis. *The Zen Truth in J.D. Salinger: It's Very Hard to Meditate and Live a Spiritual Life in America*. Northeast Missouri State University.

Grunwald, Henry Anatole, ed. 1962. *Salinger: A Critical and Personal Portrait*. New York: Harper.

Gutwillig, Robert. 1961. "Everybody's Caught *The Catcher in the Rye*." *The New York Times Paperback Review Section* 15 January, 38-39.

Gwynn, Frederick L. and Joseph L. Blotner. 1958. *The Fiction of J.D. Salinger*. Pittsburgh: University of Pittsburgh Press.

_______, ed. 1959. *Faulkner in the University. Charlottesville. Virginia.*

Hamilton, Ian. 1989. *In Search of Salinger*. London: Heinemann-Mandarin.

Harper, Howard M., Jr. 1967. *Desperate Faith: A Study of Bellow, Salinger, Mailer, Baldwin and Updike*. Chapel Hill: The University of North Carolina Press.

Harris, Charles B. 1971. *Contemporary American Novelists of the Absurd*. New Haven, Conn: College and University Press.

Hassan, Ihab. 1962. "Rare Quixotic Gesture." In Grunwald.

_______ 1961. *Radical Innocence: Studies in the Contemporary American Novel*. New York: Harper and Row.

Hauck, Richard Boyd. 1971. *A Cheerful Nihilism: Confidence and "The Absurd" in American Humorous Fiction*. Bloomington/London: Indiana University Press.

Havemann, Ernest. 1961. "The Search for the Mysterious J.D. Salinger: The Recluse in the Rye." *Life* (3 November): 129-44.

Hayes, Ann L. 1963. "J.D. Salinger: A Reputation and a Promise." in Arthur T. Broes.

Hazard, Eloise P. 1963. "Eight Fictional Finds." In Warren French.

Heidegger, Martin, 1975. "The Quest for Being." In Walter Kaufmann.

Hemingway, Ernest. 1957. *A Farwell to Arms*. New York: Charles Scribner's.

Hendin, Josephine. 1978. *Vulnerable People: A View of American Fiction Since 1945*. New York: Oxford University Press.

Heymann, C. David. 1975. "Salinger is Alive and Maybe Well and Writing." *Village Voice* (23 June): 35-42.

Hicks, Granville. "The Search for Wisdom." In Grunwald.

Hoban, Phoebe. 1987 "The Salinger File." *New York* (15 June): 36-42.

Holmes, John Clellon. 1960. "The Philosophy of the Beat Generation." In Krim.

Howe, Irving. 1969. "Mass Society and Post-Modern Fiction." In Klein.

Katz, Michael. 1971. *Class Bureaucracy and Schools*. New York: Praiger.

Kaufmann, Walter, ed. & trans. 1975. *Existentialism: From Dostoevsky to Sartre*. New York: New American Library.

Kazin, Alfred. 1973. *Bright Book of Life: American Novelists and Storytellers from Hemingway to Mailer*. Boston: Little Brown.

________. 1961. "J.D. Salinger: Everybody's Favourite." In Grunwald.

________. 1969. "The Alone Generation: A Comment on the Fiction of the 'Fifties.'" In Klein.

Kirschner, Paul. 1971. "Salinger and His Society: The Pattern of Nine Stories." *Literary Half-Yearly* 12: 2, 51-60.

Klein, Marcus, ed. 1969. *The American Novel Since World War II*. Greenwich, Connecticut: Fawcett.

Kostelanetz, Richard, ed. 1964. *On Contemporary Literature. Anthology of Critical Essays on the Major Movements and Writers of Contemporary Literature.*

Krim, Seymour, ed. 1960. *The Beats*. Greenwich: Fawcett.

Lane, Gary. 1973 "Seymour's Suicide Again: A New Reading of J.D. Salinger's 'A Perfect Day for Bananafish.'" *Studies in Short Fiction* 10:1:27-33.

Laser, Marvin and Norman Fruman, ed. 1963. *Studies in J.D. Salinger: Reviews, Essays and Critiques of The Catcher in the Rye and Other Fiction*. New York: Odyssey Press.

Leitch David. 1962. "The Salinger Myth." In Grunwald.

Levine, Paul. 1962. "J.D. Salinger: The Development of the Misfit Hero." In Belcher and Lee.

Lewis, R.W.B. 1955. *The American Adam: Innocence, Tragedy and Tradition in the Nineteenth Century*. Chicago: University of Chicago Press.

Livingston, James T. 1968. "J.D. Salinger: The Artist's Struggle to Stand on Holy Ground." In Nathan Scott 113-32.

Lodge, David. 1975. "Family Romances." *The Times Literary Supplement*, 13 June, 642.

Longstreth, T. Morris. 1963. (Review) *The Catcher in the Rye* in Laser and Fruman.

Ludwig, Jack. 1962. *Recent American Novelists.* Minneapolis: University of Minnesota Press.

Lundquist, James. 1979. *J.D. Salinger*. New York: Frederick Ungar.

Mailer, Norman. 1968. *Advertisements for Myself.* London: Panther.

_______. 1968. *The Presidential Papers*. Harmondsworth, Middlesex: Penguin.

Malin, Irving. 1962. *New American Gothic*. Carbondale: Southern Illinois University Press.

Marple, Ann 1963. "Salinger's Oasis of Innocence," in Laser and Fruman.

Marsden, Malcolm M, ed. 1963. *If You Really Want to Know: A Catcher Casebook*. Chicago: Scott, Foresman.

Maxwell, William. 1963. "J.D. Salinger." In Warren French.

McReynolds, David. 1960. "Hipsters Unleashed." In Krim.

McSweeny, K. 1978. "Salinger Revisited." *Critical Quarterly* 20: 1, 61-69.

Melville, Herman. 1962. (First Published 1851). New York: Macmillan.

Miller, James E., Jr. 1965. *J.D. Salinger*. Minneapolis: University of Minnesota Press. (Pamphlets on American Writers, No. 51).

Mitchell, Susan K. 1992. "To Tell You the Truth." *C.L.A. Journal* 36:2:145-56.

Mizener, Arthur. 1962. "The Love Song of J.D. Salinger." In Grunwald.

O'Connor, Dennis L. 1984. "J.D. Salinger's Religious Pluralism. The Example of 'Raise High the Roof Beam, Carpenters.'" *The Southern Review* 20:2.

_______. 1987. J.D. Salinger's Religious Pluralism.

Ohmann, Carol and Richard Ohmann. 1976. "Reviews, Critics and *The Catcher in the Rye*." *Critical Inquiry* 3:1:15-38.

Panichas, George A. 1974. *The Reverent Discipline: Essays in Literary Criticism and Culture*. Knoxville: University of Tennessee Press.

Park, David. 1964. *Contemporary Physics*. New York: Harcourt, Brace World.

Philips, Mark. 1985. "J.D. Salinger: A Hidden Hand?" *Saturday Review* 11:6 (November/December): 39-43.

Pillsbury, Frederick. 1961. "Mysterious J.D. Salinger: The Untold Chapter of the Famous Writer's Years as a Valley Forge Cadet." *Sunday Bulletin Magazine* (29 October): 23-24.

Pinsker, Sanford. 1993. *The Catcher in the Rye: Innocence Under Pressure.* New York: Twayne.

Piper, Henry Dan. 1962. "Modern American Classics." *Saturday Review*. (17 February): 20.

Reisman, David. 1968. *The Lonely Crowd.* In Finkelstein.

Romano, John. 1979. "Salinger Was Playing Our Game." *New York Times Book Review* (3 June): 11 and 48.
Roth, Philip. 1969. "Writing American Fiction." In Klein.
Rowe, Joyce. 1991. "Holden Caulfield and American Protest." In Jack Salzman.
Rubin, Louis D. 1973. *The Comic Imagination in American Literature*. New Jersey: Rutgers University Press.
Rupp, Richard H. 1970. *Celebration in Postwar American Fiction, 1945-1967*. Coral Gables, Florida: University of Miami Press.
Russell, John. 1966. "Salinger's Feat." *Modern Fiction Studies* 12:299-306.
Salisbury, Harrison. 1962. *New York Times*. (9 February): 4.
Salzman, Jack, ed. 1991. *New Essays on the Catcher in the Rye*. Cambridge: Cambridge University Press.
Schulz, Max F. 1969. *Radical Sophistication: Studies in Contemporary Jewish-American Novelists*. Athens: Ohio University Press.
Scott, Nathan A. Jr., ed. 1968. *Adversity and Grace: Studies in Recent American Literature*. Chicago: Universtiy of Chicago Press.
Seng, Peter J. 1961. "The Fallen Idol: The Immature World of Holden Caulfield." *College English* 23 (December): 203-9.
Sequeira, Isaac. 1975. *The Theme of Initiation in Modern American Fiction*. Mysore: Geetha Book House.
Simonson, Harold P. and Philip E. Hager, ed. 1963. *Salinger's "Catcher in the Rye": Clamor vs. Criticism*. Boston. D.C. Heath.
Skow, Jack. 1961. "Sonny: An Introduction." *Time* (15 September): 84-90.
________. 1962. "Sonny: An Introduction." In Grunwald.
Slater Philip. 1970. *The Pursuit of Loneliness*. Boston: Beacon Press.
Steiner, George. 1959. "The Salinger Industry." *The Nation* (14 November): 360-63.
Stevenson, David L. 1957. "J.D. Salinger: The Mirror of Crisis." *The Nation* (9 March): 215-17.
Strauch, Carl F. 1963. "Salinger: The Romantic Background." *Wisconsin Studies in Contemporary Literature* 4:1:31-40.
Trilling, Lionel. 1969. "Art and Fortune." In Klein.
________. 1966. "The Symbolic Structure of *The Catcher in the Rye*." *Sewanee Review* 74: 681-93.
Vandorbilt, Kermit. 1963. "Symbolic Resolution in *The Catcher in the Rye*: The Cap, the Carrousel and the American West." *Western Humanities Review* 17:3:271-77.
Vivekananda, Swami. 1955. *Karma Yoga and Bhakti Yoga*. New York: Ramakrishna Vivekananda Centre.
________. 1944. *Doctrine of Karma*. Calcutta: Ramakrishna Vedanta Math.
Wakefield, Dan 1962. "The Search for Love." In Grunwald.

Walcutt, Charles Child. 1966. *Man's Changing Mask: Modes and Methods of Characterization in Fiction*. Minneapolis. University of Minnesota Press.

Walzer, Michael. 1960. "In Place of a Hero." *Dissent* 7:2:156-67.

Wanambisi, Monica Nalyaka. 1989. Thesis. Faulkner, Salinger, Ellison, Baldwin, Marshall. Atlanta University.

Warren, Robert. 1946. *All the King's Men.* Harcourt Brace and Jovanovich.

Way, Brian. 1962. "Franny and Zooey and J.D. Salinger." *New Left Review* 15: (May-June): 72-82.

________. 1963. "A Tight Three-Movement Structure." In Laser and Fruman.

Weber, Brom. 1973. "The Mode of Black Humour." In Rubbin.

Weinberg, Helen. 1970. *The New Novel in America: The Kafkan Mode in Contemporary Fiction*. Ithaca: Cornell University Press.

Wenke, John. 1981 "Sergeant X, Esme and the Meaning of Words." *Studies in Short Fiction* 18:3:251-59.

Wexelblatt, Robert. 1986. "Chekhov, Salinger, and Epictetus." *The Midwest Quarterly* 28:50-76.

Wiegand, William. 1958. "J.D. Salinger: Seventy-Eight Bananas." *Chicago Review* 11:4:3-19.

Bibliography

Aikant, Satish C. "The Theme of Quest in Salinger's *The Catcher in the Rye*." *Kyushu American Literature*, No. 24 (July 1983), 54-59.

Aldridge, John W. *After the Lost Generation: A Critical Study of the Writers of Two Wars*. New York: McGraw Hill, 1951.

______. "The Society of Three Novels." *In Search of Heresy*: *American Literature in an Age of Conformity*. New York: McGraw Hill, 1956, 126-48.

______. *Time to Murder and Create: The Contemporary Novel in Crisis*. New York: David McKay, 1966.

Allen, Walter. *Tradition and Dream*: *The English and American Novel from the Twenties to Our Time*. London: Phoenix House, 1964.

Amur, G.S. "Theme, Structure and Symbol in *The Catcher in the Rye*." *Indian Journal of American Studies*, 1, No. 1 (1969), 11-24.

Avni, Abraham. "The Influence of the Bible on American Literature: A Review of Research from 1955 to 1965." *Bulletin of Bibliography*, 27, No. 4 (October-December 1970), 101-6.

Balakian, Nona and Charles Simmons, ed., *The Creative Present*. Garden City, New York: Doubleday, 1968.

Barr, Donald. "Should Holden Caulfield Read These Books?" *The New York Times Books Review*, 4 May 1986, 1 and 49-50.
Barron, Cynthia M. "The Catcher and the Soldier: Hemingway's 'Soldier's Home' and Salinger's *The Catcher in the Rye*." *The Hemingway Review*, 2, No. 1 (1982), 70-73.
Beach, Myrtle. "The Psychological Structure of *The Catcher in the Rye*." *PMLA*, 89, No. 5 (1974), 1065-74.
Beebe, Maurice, and Jennifer Sperry. "Criticism of J.D. Salinger: A Selected Checklist." *Modern Fiction Studies*, 12 (1966), 377-90.
Bellman, Samuel I. "New Light on Seymour's Suicide: Salinger's 'Hapworth 16, 1924.'" *Studies in Short Fiction*, 3, No. 3 (1966), 348-51.
________. "Peripheral (?) Characters in *Huckleberry Finn* and *Catcher in the Rye*." *Mark Twain Journal*, 19, No. 1 (1977-78), 4-6.
"Bid for Salinger." *Observer* (London), 26 November 1961.
Blotner, Joseph L. "Salinger Now: An Appraisal." *Wisconsin Studies in Contemporary Literature*, 4, No. 1 (1963) 100-8.
Bowen, Robert O. "The Salinger Syndrome: Charity against Whom?" *Ramparts*, 1 (May 1962), 52-60.
Boyle, Robert S.J. "Teaching 'Dirty Books' in College." *America*, 13 December 1958, 337-39.
Brandon, Henry. "A Conversation with Edmund Wilson: 'We Don't Know Where We Are.'" *The New Republic*, 30 March 1959, 13-15.
Breslow, Paul. "The Support of the Mysteries: A Look at the Literary Prophets of the Beat Middle Class." *Studies on the Left* (Madison, Wisconsin), 1 (Fall 1959), 15-28.
Brickell, Herschel. "J.D. Salinger." *Prize Stories of 1949: The O'Henry Awards*, ed. Herschel Brickell. Garden City, New York: Doubleday, 1950, 249.
Brinkley, Thomas Edwin. "J.D. Salinger: A Study of His Eclecticism—Zooey as Existential Zen Therapist." Diss. The Ohio State University, 1976, *DAI* 37; 7127A.
Browne, Robert M. "In Defense of Esme." *College English*, 22 (May 1961), 584-85.
Bryan, James. "The Admiral and Her Sailor in Salinger's 'Down at the Dinghy.'" *Studies in Short Fiction*, 17 No. 2 (1980), 174-78.
________. "Salinger's Seymour's Suicide." *College English*, 24 (December 1962), 226-29.
________. "J.D. Salinger: The Fat Lady and the Chicken Sandwich." *College English*, 23 (December 1961), 226-29.
________. "A Reading of Salinger's 'Teddy.'" *American Literature*, 40 No. 3 (1968), 352-69.
________. "The Psychological Structure of *The Catcher in the Rye*." *PMLA*, 89 (October 1974), 1065-74.
Burack, Boris. "Holden the Courageous." *CEA Critic*, 27:8 (1965), 1.
Burgess, Anthony. "The Postwar American Novel: A View from the Pe-

riphery." *The American Scholar*, 35:1 (1965-66), 150-56.

Burke, Brother Fidelian. "Salinger's Esme: Some Matters of Balance." *Modern Fiction Studies*, 12 (1966), 341-47.

Cagle, Charles. "*The Catcher in the Rye* Revisited." *Midwest Quarterly*, 4, No. 4 (1963), 343-51.

Carpenter, Frederic I. "The Adolescent in American Fiction." *The English Journal*, 46, No. 6 (1957), 313-19.

________. "The Characteristic Form: A Distinct Predilection for the Short Story." *The Times Literary Supplement*, 6 November 1959, xv.

Coles, R. "J.D. Salinger: A Return Look at *Catcher in the Rye* and *Franny and Zooey*." *New Republic*, 28 April 1973, 30-32.

________. "Contributors." *Story*, 16 (March-April 1940), 2.

________. "Contributors." *Story*, 21 (September-October 1942), 2.

________. "Contributors." *Story*, 25 (November-December 1944), 1.

________. "Contributors." *Story*, 26 (March-April 1945), 4.

Corbett, Edward P.J. "Some Thoughts on *The Catcher in the Rye*: Raise High the Barriers, Censors." *America*, 7 January 1961, 441-43.

Corkery, P. (illustrated portraits). "Solitude May be Bliss for Author J.D. Salinger, But To Son Matt. All the World's A Stage." *People*, 31 October 1983, 111-12.

Costello, D.P. "The Language of *The Catcher in the Rye*." *American Speech*, 34 (October 1959), 172-81.

________. "Salinger and His Critics." (illustrated) *Commonweal*, 25 October 1963, 132-35.

Cotter, James Finn. "Religious Symbols in Salinger's Shorter Fiction." *Studies in Short Fiction*, 15, No. 2 (1978), 121-32.

Cox, James M. "Toward Vernacular Humor." *Virginia Quarterly Review*, 46, No. 2 (1970), 311-30.

Cunliffe, Marcus. *The Literature of the United States*. Baltimore: Penguin, 1961, 346-47, 364.

D'Avanzo, Mario L. "Gatsby and Holden Caulfield." *Fitzgerald Newsletter*, No. 38 (Summer 1967), 4-6.

Dahl, James. "What about Antolini?" *Notes on Contemporary Literature*, 13, No. 2 (1983), 9-10.

Davis, Tom. "J.D. Salinger: The Identity of Sergeant X." *Western Humanities Review*, 16, No. 2 (1962), 181-83.

________. "J.D. Salinger: 'Some Crazy Cliff' Indeed." *Western Humanities Review*, 14 (1960), 97-99.

Davison, Richard Allan. "Salinger Criticism and 'The Laughing Man': A Case of Arrested Development." *Studies in Short Fiction*, 18, No. 1 (1981), 1-15.

Delbanco, Andrew. "Holden Caulfield Goes to Law School." *The New Republic*, 9 March 1987, 27-30.

Dempsey, D. "Secret of Seymour and Esme" (illustrated) *Saturday Review*, 30 June 1962, 19.

Detweiler, Robert. *Four Spiritual Crises in Mid-Century Fiction.* Gainesville, Florida: University of Florida Press, 1963. (University of Florida Monographs; Humanities No. 14)

Dodge, Stewart. "In Search of 'The Fat Lady.'" *The English Record*, New York State English Council, Genesco, 8 (Winter 1957), 10-13.

Drake, Robert Y. Jr. "Two Old Juveniles." *The Georgia Review*, 13 (Winter 1959), 443-53.

Ducharme, Edward. "J.D., Sonny, Sunny, and Holden." *English Record*, 19 (1968), 54-58.

"Early Excursions into Glass Country." *The Times Literary Supplement*, 8 April 1960, 228.

Ely, Sister M. and O.P. Amanda. "The Adult Image in Three Novels of Adolescent Life." *English Journal*, 56 (November 1967), 1127-31.

Ely, M. "Cup of Consecrated Chicken Soup." *Catholic World*, 202 (February 1966), 298-301.

Erwin, Kenneth J. "An Analysis of the Dramatic and Semantic Use of Altruism in the Writings of J.D. Salinger." Diss. Texas, Austin 29 (1968), *DAI* 1535-36A.

Faulkner, William. "A Word to Young Writers," in Frederich L. Gwynn and Joseph L. Blotner, ed., *Faulkner in the University: Class Conferences at the University of Virginia, 1957-1958.* Charlottesville: The University of Virginia Press, 1959, 241-45.

Feinstein Herbert. "Contemporary American Fiction: Harvey Swados and Leslie Fiedler." *Wisconsin Studies in Contemporary Literature*, No. 1 (1960-61), 79-98.

Fenton, Charles. "Lost Years of Twentieth Century American Literature." *The South Atlantic Quarterly*, 59 (September 1960), 332-38.

Fiedler, Leslie A. "The Un-Angry Young Men." *Encounter* (London), 10 January 1958, 3-12.

________. "The Invention of the Child." *The New Leader*, 31 March, 1958, 22-24.

________. "Good Girl and Good Bad Boy." *The New Leader*, 14 April 1958, 22-25.

________. "Boys Will Be Boys." *The New Leader*, 28 April 1958, 23-26.

________. "The Profanation of the Child." *The New Leader*, 23 June 1958, 26-29.

________. *Love and Death in the American Novel.* New York: Criterion, 1960, see Chapters 8 and 9.

________. "From Redemption to Initiation." *The New Leader*, 26 May 1958, 20-23.

Fiene, Donald M. "J.D. Salinger: A Bibliography." *Wisconsin Studies in Contemporary Literature*, 4, No. 1 (1963), 109-49.

________. "From a Study of Salinger: Controversy in the *Catcher*." *The Realist* (New York), No. 30 (December 1961), 1, 23-25.

Fleissner, Robert F. "Salinger's Caulfield: A Refraction of Copperfield and His Caul." *Notes on Contemporary Literature*, 3 (1973), 5-7.

Fogel, Amy. "Where the Ducks Go: *The Catcher in the Rye.*" *Ball State Teacher's College Forum*, 3 (Spring 1962), 75-79.

Foran, Donald J. "A Doubletake on Holden Caulfield." *English Journal*, 57, No. 7 (1968), 977-79.

Fowler, Albert. "Alien in the Rye." *Modern Age: A Conservative Review*, 1 (Fall 1957), 193-97.

Friedrich, Gerhard. "Perspective in the Teaching of American Literature." *College English*, 20 (December 1958), 122-28.

Furst, Lilian R. "Dostoyevsky's Notes from Underground and Salinger's *The Catcher in the Rye.*" *Canadian Review of Comparative Literature*, 5 (1978), 72-85.

Gehman, Richard. "Introduction." *The Best from Cosmopolitan*, ed. Richard Gehman, New York: Avon, 1961, xiii-xxvii.

Genthe, Charles V. "Six, Sex, Sick: Seymour, Some Comments." *Twentieth Century Literature*. 10 (April 1964-January 1965), 170-71.

Giles, Barbara. "The Lonely War of J.D. Salinger." *Mainstream* (New York), 12 (February 1959), 2-13.

Glazier, Lyle. *Decadence and Rebirth*: Hacettepe Lectures in American Literature. Ankara: Hacettepe University Publications, 1971.

________. "The Glass Family Saga: Argument and Epiphany." *College English*, 27 (December 1965), 248-51.

Gold, Herbert. "Fiction of the Sixties." *The Atlantic*, 206 (September 1960), 53-57.

Goldhurst, William. "The Hyphenated Ham Sandwich of Ernest Hemingway and J.D. Salinger: A Study in Literary Continuity." *Fitzgerald/Hemingway Annual* (1970), 136-50.

Goldstein, Bernice and Sanford Goldstein. "Zen and Salinger." *Modern Fiction Studies*, 12 (1966), 313-24.

________. "'Seymour: An Introduction'—Writing as Discovery." *Studies in Short Fiction*, 7 (Spring 1970), 248-56.

________. "Bunnies and Cobras: Zen Enlightenment in Salinger." *Discourse*, 13 (1970), 98-106.

________. "Zen and *Nine Stories.*" *Rehascence*, 22 (1970), 171-82.

________. "Some Zen References in Salinger." *Literature East and West*, 15 (1971), 83-95.

________. "Ego and 'Hapworth 16, 1924.'" *Renascence*, 24 (1972), 159-67.

________. "Seymour's Poems." *Literature East and West*, 17 (1973), 335-48.

Goodner, R.D. "One of Today's Best Little Writers?" *Cambridge Quarterly* (Winter 1965/66), 81-90.

Green, Martin. "Amis and Salinger: The Latitude of Private Conscience." *Chicago Review*, 11, No. 4 (1958), 20-25.

________. "Cultural Images in England and America." *A Mirror for An-*

glo-Saxons: A Discovery of America, A Rediscovery of England. New York: Harper, 1960, 69-88.

________. "Re-Appraisals: *Some Commonsense Readings of American Literature*. New York: Norton, 1963, 197-229.

Gross, Theodore L. "J.D. Salinger: Suicide and Survival in the Modern World." *South Atlantic Quarterly*, 68, No. 4 (1969), 454-62.

Grunwald, Henry Anatole. "He Touches Something Deep in Us." *Horizon* (New York) 4 (May 1962), 100-7.

Guirao, John N. "*Catcher in the Rye*." *Kyushu American Literature*, No. 7 (April 1964), 5-12.

Hagopian, John V. "Pretty Mouth and Green My Eyes." *Modern Fiction Studies*, 12 (1966), 349-54.

Hainsworth, J.D. "Maturity in J.D. Salinger's 'The Catcher in the Rye.'" *English Studies*, 48 (October 1967), 426-31.

Hamilton, Kenneth. *J.D. Salinger: A Critical Essay*. Grand Rapids: William B. Eerdmans, 1967.

________. "Hell in New York: J.D. Salinger's 'Pretty Mouth and Green My Eyes.'" *Dalhousie Review*, 47, No. 3 (1967), 394-99.

Handa, Takuya. "On Interpretation of J.D. Salinger's *The Catcher in the Rye*." *Kyushu American Literature*, No. 21 (June 1980), 42-53.

Hardy, John Edward. "J.D. Salinger: 'Down at the Dinghy." *Commentaries on Five Modern American Short Stories*. Frankfurt-am-Main (and Berlin, Bonn): Verlag Moritz Diesterweg, 1962, 7-10.

Hassan, Ihab. "The Idea of Adolescence in American Fiction." *American Quarterly*, 10 (1958), 312-24.

________. "The Victim: Images of Evil in Recent American Fiction." *College English*, 21 (December 1959), 140-46.

________. "The Character of Post-War Fiction in America." *The English Journal*, 51 (January 1962), 1-8.

________. "Almost the Voice of Silence: The Later Novelettes of J.D. Salinger." *Wisconsin Studies in Contemporary Literature*, 4, No. 1 (1963), 5-20.

Hayman, June. "The White Jew." *Dissent*, 8 (Spring 1961), 191-96.

Heiney, Donald W. *Recent American Literature*. Great Neck, New York: Barron's, 1958, 281-84.

Heiserman, Arthur, and James E. Miller, Jr. "J.D. Salinger, Some Crazy Cliff." *Western Humanities Review* 10 (Spring 1956), 129-37.

Hermann, John. "J.D. Salinger: Hello, Hello, Hello." *College English*, 22 (January 1961), 262-64.

Hicks, Granville. "Quest in a Quiet Time." *Saturday Review*, 28 November 1959, 20.

________. "Another Look at the Deserving." *Saturday Review*, 23 December 1961, 18.

________. "Sisters, Sons and Lovers." *Saturday Review*, 16 September 1961, 26.

Hinckle, Warren. "J.D. Salinger's Glass Menagerie." *Ramparts*, 1 (May 1962), 48-51.

Horton, Rod W. and Herbert W. Edwards. *Background of American Literary Thought*. New York: Appleton-Century-Crofts, 1952.

Howell, John M. "Salinger in the Waste Land." *Modern Fiction Studies*, 12 (1966), 367-75.

Huber, R.J. "Adlerian Theory and Its Application to *The Catcher in the Rye*—Holden Caulfield." 43-52 in Joseph Natoli, ed., *Psychological Perspectives on Literature: Freudian Dissidents and Non-Freudians: A Casebook*. Hamdon, CT: Archon, 1984, vii, 288.

Hutchens, John K. "On an Author." *The New York Herald Tribune Book Review*, 19 August 1951, 2.

Jacobs, Robert G. "J.D. Salinger's *The Catcher in the Rye*: Holden Caulfield's 'Goddam Autobiography.'" *Iowa English Yearbook* (Fall 1959), 9-14.

Jacobsen, Josephine. "Beatific Signals: The Felicity of J.D. Salinger." *Commonweal,* 26 February 1960, 589-91.

"J.D. Salinger—Biographical." *Harper's*, 218 (February 1959), 87.

Johannson, Ernest J. "Salinger's Seymour." *The Carolina Quarterly*, 7 (Winter 1959), 51-54.

Johnson, William. "The Zen Enlightenment." *Thought*, 42, No. 165 (Summer 1967), 165-84.

Johnson, James W. "The Adolescent Hero: A Trend in Modern Fiction." *Twentieth Century Literature*, 5 (April 1959), 3-11.

Jones, Ernest. "Case History of All of Us." *The Nation*, 1 September 1951, 176.

Kaplan, Charles. "Holden and Huck: The Odysseys of Youth." *College English*, 18 (November 1956), 76-80.

Karl, Frederick R. *American Fictions, 1940-1980: A Comprehensive History of Critical Evaluations*. New York: Harper and Row, 1985.

Karlistetter, Karl. "J.D. Salinger, R.W. Emerson and the Perennial Philosophy." *Modern Sprak*, 63 (1969), 224-36.

Keating, Edward M. "Salinger: The Murky Mirror." *Ramparts*, 1 (May 1962), 61-66.

"Keeping Posted: A Thin Slice of College." *The Saturday Evening Post*, 15 April 1944, 4.

Kegel, Charles H. "Incommunicability in Salinger's *The Catcher in the Rye*." *Western Humanities Review*, 11 (Spring 1957), 188-90.

Kermode, Frank. "Fit Audience." *The Spectator* (London), 30 May 1958, 705-6.

Kim, Chong-Un. "The Novels of J.D. Salinger." *English Language and Literature*, 18 (June 1960), 107-19.

Kinney, Arthur F. "J.D. Salinger and the Search for Love." *Texas Studies in Literature and Language*, 5 (Spring 1963), 11-126.

Kirschner, Paul. "Salinger and His Society: The Pattern of Nine Stories."

Literary Half Yearly, 14, No. 2 (1973), 63-78.
Klein, Marcus. *After Alienation: American Novels in Mid-Century*. Cleveland & New York: The World Publishing Co., 1965.
Kosner, Edward. "The Private World of J.D. Salinger." *New York Post Week End Magazine*, 30 April 1961, 5.
Kranidas, Thomas. "Point of View in Salinger's 'Teddy.' *Studies in Short Fiction*, 2 (Fall 1964), 89-91.
Krassner, Paul. "What Makes Critics Happy?" *The Realist*, No. 14 (December-January 1959-1960), 5-6.
________. "The Age of Form Letters." *The Realist*, No. 15 (February 1960), 6.
________. "An Impolite Interview with Alan Watts." *The Realist*, No. 14 (December 1960), 1, 8-11.
Kumar, Anil. "Alienation in the Fiction of Carson McCullers, J.D. Salinger and James Purdy." Thesis. Amritsar: Guru Nanak Dev University, 1982.
Larner, Jeremy. "Salinger's Audience: An Explanation." *Partisan Review*, 29, No. 4 (1962), 594-98.
Lerman, Leo. "It Takes 4." *Madmemoiselle*, 53 (October 1961), 108-9.
Leverett, Ernest. "The Virtues of Vulgarity—Russian and American Views." *The Carleton Miscellany*, 1 (Spring 1960), 29-40.
Levin, Beatrice. "J.D. Salinger in Oklahoma." *Chicago Jewish Forum*, 19 (Spring 1961), 231-33.
________. "Everybody's Favorite: Concepts of Love in the Work of J.D. Salinger." *Motive* (Nashville, Tenn.) 22 (October 1961), 9-11.
Lewis, Roger. "Textual Variants in J.D. Salinger's *Nine Stories*." *Resources for American Literature*, No. 1 (1980), 79-83.
Lewis, R.W.B. "American Letters: A Projection." *The Yale Review*, 51, No. 2 (1961), 211-26.
Light, James F. "Salinger's *The Catcher in the Rye*." *Explicator*, 18 (June 1960), Item 59.
"The Limits of the Possible: Accepting the Reality of the Human Situation." *The Times Literary Supplement*, 6 (November 1959), xvi.
Lipton, Lawrence. "Disaffiliation and the Art of Poverty." *Chicago Review*, 10, No. 1 (1956), 53-79.
Lorch, Thomas M. "J.D. Salinger: The Artist, the Audience, and the Popular Arts." *South Dakota Review*, 4 (1967-68), 3-13.
Love, Glen A. "Ecology in Arcadia." *Colorado Quarterly*, 21, No. 2 (1972), 175-85.
Lowrey, Burling. "Salinger and the House of Glass." *The New Republic*, 26 October 1959, 23-24.
Luedtke, Luther S. "J.D. Salinger and Robert Burns: *The Catcher in the Rye*." *Modern Fiction Studies*, 16 (1970), 198-201.
Lyons, John O. "The Romantic Style of Salinger's 'Seymour: Introduction.'" *Wisconsin Studies in Contemporary Literature*, 4 (Winter

1963), 62-69.

Maclean, Hugh. "Conservatism in Modern American Fiction." *College English*, 15 (March 1954), 315-25.

Marcus, Fred H. "*The Catcher in the Rye*: A Live Circuit." *English Journal*, 52, No. 1 (1963), 1-8.

Margolis, John D. "The Place of Love in Society: Salinger's Heroes." *The Haverford News*, 9 February 1962, 2.

________. "Salinger's *The Catcher in the Rye*." *Explicator* 22 (November 1963), No. 23.

Marks, Barry A., Donald H. Reiman and Dexter Martin. "Rebuttal: Holden in the Rye." *College English*, 23 (May 1962), 507-8.

Martin, Augustin. "A Note on J.D. Salinger." *Studies: An Irish Quarterly Review*, 48 (Fall 1959), 336-45.

Martin, H. "The American Problem of Direct Address." *Western Humanities Review*, 16 (Winter 1952), 101-14.

Mathis, Jim. "'The Catcher in the Rye': Controversy on the Novel in Texas Is Just One in Long List of Episodes." *The Houston Post*, 4 May 1961, Section 7, 6.

Matthews, James F. "J.D. Salinger: An Appraisal." *University of Virginia Magazine*, 1 (Spring 1956), 52-60.

Maxwell, William. "J.D. Salinger." *The Book-of-the-Month Club News* (July 1951), 5-6.

May, John R. *Toward a New Earth: Apocalypse in the American Novel*. Notre Dame, London: University of Notre Dame Press, 1972.

McCarthy, Mary. "Characters in Fiction." *The Partisan Review*, 28, No. 2 (1961), 171-91.

________. "J.D. Salinger's Closed Circuit." *Harper's* 225 (October 1962), 45-48.

McConnell, Frank D. *Four Postwar American Novelists: Bellow, Mailer, Barth and Pynchon*. Chicago: The University of Chicago Press, 1977.

McIntyre, John P., S.J. "A Preface for 'Franny and Zooey,'" *The Critic* 20 (February-March 1962), 25-28.

McNamara, Eugene. "Holden as Novelist." *English Journal*, 54, No. 3 (1965), 166-70.

Meral, Jean. "The Ambiguous Mr. Antolini in Salinger's *The Catcher in the Rye*." *Caliban*, 7 (1970) 55-58.

Metcalf, Frank. "The Suicide of Salinger's Seymour Glass." *Studies in Short Fiction*, 9 (1972), 243-46.

Miller, Erwin Haviland. "In Memorium: Allie Caulfield in *The Catcher in the Rye*." *Mosaic*, 15 (Winter 1982), 129-40.

Miller, James E., Jr. "Catcher in and out of History." *Critical Inquiry*, 3, No. 3 (1977), 599-603.

Milton, John R. "The American Novel: The Search for Home, Tradition and Identity." *Western Humanities Review* 16, No. 2 (1962), 169-80.

Mirza, Humayun Ali. "The Influence of Hindu-Buddhist Psychology and Philosophy on J.D. Salinger's Fiction." Diss. State University of New York at Binghampton, 1976, *DAI*, 37; 971-A.

Mizener, Arthur. "The American Hero as Poet: Seymour Glass." *The Sense of Life in the Modern Novel*. Boston: Houghton Mifflin, 1954, 227-46.

Moore, Harry T., ed., *Contemporary American Novelists*. Carbondale: Southern Illinois University Press, 1964.

Moore, Robert P. "The World of Holden." *English Journal*, 54, No. 3 (1965), 159-65.

Noguchi, Kenji. "The Function of the First Person Narrator in *The Great Gatsby* and *The Catcher in the Rye*." *Kyushu American Literature*, No. 24 (July 1983), 72-73.

Noland, Richard W. "The Novel of Personal Formula: J.D. Salinger." *University Review*, 33 (October 1966), 19-24.

"The No-Nonsense Kids." *Time*, 18 November 1957, 51-54.

O'Hara, J.D. "No Catcher in the Rye," in Max Westbrook, ed., *The Modern American Novel: Essays in Criticism*. New York: Random House, 1966, 211-20.

Ohmann, Carol and Richard Ohmann. "Universals and the Historically Particular." *Critical Inquiry*, 3 No. 4 (1977), 773-77.

Oldsey, Bernard S. "The Movies in the Rye." *College English*, 23 (December 1961), 209-15.

Orel, Harold. "What They Think About Teen-Agers in Books." *College English*, 23 (November 1961), 147-49.

Paniker, Sumitra. "The Influence of Eastern Thought on 'Teddy' and the Seymour Glass Stories of J.D. Salinger." Diss. The University of Texas at Austin, 1971. *DAI*, 32; 6446A-47A.

Parish Michael E. "Seymour: A Postscript." *Commentary*, 36, No. 5 (1963), 350.

Peavy, Charles D. "'Did You Ever Have a Sister?' Holden, Quentin, and Sexual Innocence." *Florida Quarterly*, 1 (1968), 82-95.

________. "Holden's Courage Again." *CEA Critic*, 28, No. 1 (1965), 1, 6, 9.

Perrine, Laurence. "Teddy? Booper? or Blooper?" *Studies in Short Fiction*, 4, No. 3 (1967), 217-24.

"Personal and Otherwise." *Harper's*, 198 (April 1949), 9-10.

Phelps, Robert. "Salinger: A Man of Fierce Privacy." *New York Herald Tribune Books*, 17 September 1961, 3.

Pickering, John Kenneth. "J.D. Salinger: Portraits of Alienation." Diss. Western Reserve University, 1968. *DAI*, 30; 3954A.

Piwinski, David J. "Salinger's 'De Daumier-Smith's Blue Period': Pseudonym as Cryptogram." *Notes on Contemporary Literature*, 15 (November 1985), 3-4.

Proffer, Carl R. ed. and trans. *Soviet Criticism of American Literature:*

An Anthology. Ann Arbor: Ardis, 1972, 4-14.

Quagliano, Anthony. "Hapworth 16, 1924: A Problem in Hagiography." *University of Dayton Review*, 8, No. 2 (1971), 35-43.

Ranly, Ernest W. "Journey to the East." *Commonweal*, 23 February 1973, 465-69.

Reiman, Donald H. "Salinger's *The Catcher in the Rye*." *Explicator*, 21 (March 1963), No. 58.

Romanova, Elena. "Reviews and News: What American Novels Do Russians Read?" *Soviet Literature*, No. 7 (July 1961), 178-82.

Rose, Alan Henry. "Sin and the City: The Uses of Disorder in the Urban Novel." *Centennial Review*, 16, No. 3 (1972), 203-20.

Rosen, Gerald. "A Retrospective Look at *The Catcher in the Rye*." *American Quarterly*, 29 (1977), 547-62.

Rovit, Earl H. "The Ambiguous Modern Novel." *The Yale Review*, 49, No. 2 (1960), 413-24.

Rubin, Louis D. "Don Quixote and Selected Progeny: Or the Journeyman as Outsider." *Southern Review*, 10 (January 1974), 31-58.

Russell, John. "Salinger, from Daumier to Smith," *Wisconsin Studies in Contemporary Literature*, 4, No. 1 (1963), 70-87.

"Salinger: An Introduction." *Christian Century*, 27 February 1963, 287.

Schrader, Allen. "Emerson to Salinger to Parker." *Saturday Review*, 11 April 1959, 52, 58.

Schulz, Max F. "Epilogue to Seymour: An Introduction and the Crisis of Consciousness." *Studies in Short Fiction*, 5, No. 2 (1968), 128-38.

Schwart, Arthur. "For Seymour With Love and Judgement." *Wisconsin Studies in Contemporary Literature*, 4, No. 1 (1963), 88-89.

Seitzman, Daniel. "Therapy and Antitherapy in Salinger's Zooey." *American Imago*, 25, No. 2 (1968), 140-62.

Severin-Lounsberry, Barbara. "Holden and Alex: A Clockwork from the Rye?" *Four Quarters* (Summer 1973), 27-38.

Simms, Moody, Jr. "Seymour Glass: The Salingerian Hero as Vulgarian." *Notes on Contemporary Literature*, 5, No. 3 (1975), 6-8.

Slabey, Robert M. "Sergeant X and Seymour Glass." *Western Humanities Review*, 16, No. 4 (1962), 376-77.

________. "*The Catcher in the Rye*: Christian Theme and Symbol." *CLA Journal*, 6, No. 3 (1963), 170-83.

Slavitt, David R. "Poetry, Novels and Critics: A Reply." *The Yale Review*, 51 (Spring 1962), 502-4.

Slethaug, Gordon E. "Form in Salinger's Shorter Fiction." *Canadian Review of American Studies*, 3 (Spring 1972), 50-59.

Smith, Harrison. "Manhattan Ulysses, Junior." *Saturday Review*, 14 July 1951, 12-13.

Spanier, Sandra Whipple. "Hemingway's 'The Last Good Country' and *The Catcher in the Rye*: More Than a Family Resemblance." *Studies*

in Short Fiction, 19, No. 1 (1982), 35-43.
Stein, William Bysshe. "Salinger's 'Teddy': Tat Twam Asi: or That Thou Art." *The Arizona Quarterly*, 29, No. 1 (1973), 253-65.
Stern, James. "Aw, the World's a Crumby Place." *New York Times Book Review*, 15 July 1951, 5.
Stone, Edward. "Salinger's Carrousel." *Modern Fiction Studies*, 13 (1967-68), 520-23.
________. "Naming in Salinger." *Notes on Contemporary Literature*, 1, No. 2 (1971), 2-3.
Strauch, Carl F. "Kings in the Back Row: Meaning through Structure—A Reading of Salinger's *The Catcher in the Rye*." *Wisconsin Studies in Contemporary Literature*, 2 (Winter 1961), 5-30.
Straumann, Heinrich, *American Literature in the Twentieth Century*. 3rd edn. rev. New York: Harper and Row, 1965.
Stuart, Robert Lee. "The Writer-in-Waiting." *Christian Century*, 19 May 1965, 647-49.
Sublette, Jack R. *J.D. Salinger: An Annotated Bibliography, 1938-1981* New York: Garland, 1984.
Swados, Harvey. "Must Writers Be Characters?" *Saturday Review*, 1 October 1960, 12-14, 58.
Swinton, John. "A Case Study of an 'Academic Bum': Salinger Once Stayed at Ursinus." *The Ursinus Weekly*, 12 December 1960, 2, 4.
Tanner, Tony. *City of Words: American Fiction, 1950-1970*. New York: Harper and Row, 1971.
Tarinaya, M. "Salinger: *The Catcher in the Rye*." *Literary Half-Yearly*, 7, No. 2 (1966), 49-60.
Tick, Stanley. "Initiation In and Out: The American Novel and the American Dream." *The Quadrant* (Sydney, Australia), (1961), 63-74.
Tierce, Mike. "Salinger's 'De Daumier Smith's Blue Period.'" 42 (Fall 1983), 56-58.
________. "Salinger's 'For Esme—With Love and Squalor.'" *Explicator*, 42 (Spring 1984), 56-58.
Tirumalal, Candadai K. "Salinger's *The Catcher in the Rye*." *Explicator*, 22 (March 1964), No. 56.
Tosta, Michael R. "Will the Real Sergeant X Please Stand Up?" *Western Humanities Review*, 16, No. 4 (1962), 76-77.
Toynbee, Philip. "Experiment and the Future of the Novel." in John Lehman, ed., *The Craft of Letters in England*. London: Cresset, 1956, 60-73.
Travis, Mildred K. "About *The Catcher*." *Explicator*, 21 (December 1962), No. 36.
Trilling, Lionel. "Lord of the Flies." *The Midcentury*, No. 45 (October 1962), 10-12.
Trowbridge, Clinton W. "Hamlet and Holden." *English Journal*, 57, No. 1 (1968), 26-29.

_______. "Salinger's Symbolic Use of Character and Detail in *The Catcher in the Rye*." *Cimarron Review*, 4 (June 1968), 5-11.

Vail, D. "Holden and Psychoanalysis." *PMLA*, 91 (January 1976), 120-21.

Vogel, Albert W. "J.D. Salinger on Education." *School and Society*, 91 (Summer 1963), 240-42.

Wakefield, Dan. "The Heavy Hand of College Humor: Superman, Sex and Salinger." *Mademoiselle*, 55 (August 1962), 288-89, 341-43.

Walter, Eugene. "A Rainy Afternoon with Truman Capote." *Intro Bulletin* (December 1957), 1, 2.

Weals, Gerald. "The Not So Modern Temper." *The Antioch Review*. 17 (December 1957), 510-15.

Weatherby, W.J. "J.D." *The Guardian* (Manchester) 15 January 1960, 8.

_______. "Rejection World," *Twentieth Century*, 171 (Spring 1962), 74-75.

Wells, Arvin. R. "Huck Finn and Holden Caulfield: The Situation of the Hero." *Ohio University Review*, 2 (1960), 31-42.

West, Ray B. Jr. *The Short Story in America*. Chicago: Henry Regnery, 1952, 120.

Weston, Jessie L. *From Ritual to Romance*. Garden City, New York: Doubleday, 1957.

Whittemore, Reed. "But Seriously." *The Carleton Miscellany*, 3 (Spring 1962), 58-76.

Widmer, Kingsley. "Poetic Naturalism in the Contemporary Novel." *The Partisan Review*, 26 (Summer 1959), 467-72.

_______. "The American Road: The Contemporary Novel." *University of Kansas City Review*, 26 (June 1960), 309-17.

Wiegand, William. "The Knighthood of J.D. Salinger." *The New Republic*, 19 October 1959, 19-21.

_______. "Salinger and Kierkegaard." *Minnesota Review*, 5, No. 2 (May-July 1965), 137-56.

Willeford, Charles. "Notes on Beat Writing." *The Chicago Jewish Forum*, 19 (Spring 1961), 234-37.

Wilson, John F. "The Step Beyond." *Saturday Review*, 15 August 1959, 21.

Index